Lunar Nodes:
New Concepts

Bernice Prill Grebner

Copyright 1980 by American Federation of Astrologers, Inc.
All rights reserved.

No part of this book may be reproduced or transmitted in any form or by any means, electronic or mechanical, including photocopying or recording, or by any information storage and retrieval system, without written permission from the author and publisher. Requests and inquiries may be mailed to: American Federation of Astrologers, Inc., PO Box 22040, Tempe, AZ 85284-2040.

ISBN-10: 0-86690-186-8
ISBN-13: 978-0-86690-
LCC: 76-23538

First Printing: 1980
Ninth Printing: 2006

Cover Design: Jack Cipolla

Published by:
American Federation of Astrologers, Inc.
6535 S. Rural Road
Tempe, AZ 85283

Printed in the United States of America

Prologue

The fear of what I must learn
Is tucked away
In some musty corner of my brain,
Right next to the evil smile
Of your memory.

Only when my self-assurance flickers low
Like a campfire in the rain
Do my teachers wander from the darkness,
And circle my shelter in wolf packs,
Flooding my soul with blood
With their tiny dagger eyes.

As I lie wounded through the long night,
The memory of soft eyes
And gentle hands
Burns my skin like acid,
And what little strength I have left
Is wasted chasing your phantom.

By morning the pain has burned itself out
And I feel sterilized.
Your image had fled,
And my teachers have stopped nagging,
No buzzards will come now…
But your image may knock on my door,
Once again,
And I may be called on to recite my lessons
Once again.

David Grebner

The person who is aware of his destiny

is the richest person

in the world

Dedicated to the eternal Sweet Prince!

Contents

Introduction	ix
Karma	xv
South Node Heritage	xv
Relationships	xv
South Node through the Houses	1
North Node through the Houses	7
Comments	13
Aspects to the Nodes	17
Why Failure at the South Node?	27
Nodal Dignities and Debilities	29
Transits	31
Progressions	35
Astronomical Explanation of the Nodes	41
Nodal Points in the Charts of Famous People	43
Synastry Aspects	51
Synastry Interpretation	61
Conclusion	65
Appendices	
1, Nodal Theories	67
2, Current Transiting Nodes	69
3, Lunar Nodal Return	71
4, Additional Thoughts on the Nodes	73
5, Past Lives or Vocations Taking Little Effort	79
6, Needs for Release	81
7, Examples	83
8, Location of North and South Nodes	85
9, Newer Information on the Lunar Nodes	91

Introduction

Are your Nodes balanced yet? This is what must be done!

It is much easier to continue at the South Node than to come to the North Node area. One pushes and struggles at the North Node area where the new growth must be worked for. Whenever anything goes wrong in one's life, the person wants to revert to the South Node position where he is safe and secure.

When one is very young, the earliest memories are of a shyness in the area of the North Node, regardless of the aspects to it. It is a new area, like a new land. We must learn our way, groping in the dark as lost children in a new age. Aspects to this North Node indicate how we are to obtain this new growth, our struggles with it, the obstacles, and ultimate benefits.

We are talking about a relationship between the plane of the Moon's orbit and that of the Earth's orbit. The Earth's orbit centers around the Sun as do the other planets, but the Moon's orbit goes around the Earth. It is the meeting of these two planes that produces the North and South Nodes. This relationship between the two orbits becomes the relation of Earth to Sun. This means an adjustment of our Earth-centered ego and our own self-will with that if the solar self, or cosmic will. The Moon navigates its orbit of the Earth each month. The Earth is moving around the Sun at the same time. At one time the Moon goes to the north of the ecliptic; at the other time to the south. The first crossing is called the North Node; the return is called the South Node. Light focalizes or singularizes at the North Node, and scatters or spreads at the South Node. Thus at the South Node in our charts we should extend our knowledge in many directions or to many people, instead of possessively holding it to us.

The axis, or line, of the nodes show us the direction of our destiny. The North Node shows a new learning; the South Node shows that which is instinctive, or well known. Now, let us consider the South Node in Aries in the fifth house. We are considering love, creativity, children, pleasure, relating it to Aries. We find the self, the single unit, the leader, the pioneer of love, dealing with children, creativity, and pleasure. This is the knowledgeable area where there is more of a chance for genius. This person with the South Node in Aries has great self-sufficiency. This is also true of the South Node in the first house.

Consider the South Node in Libra in the fifth house. Here again we have love, pleasure, children, and creativity. Coupled with Libra, which is partnership, we have one who considers the partner first, almost to his detriment. This is the person who needs a partner very much, to operate efficiently in this area.

The South Node area constantly seems to change, or is in danger of being destroyed in some way. With South Node in Aries, it is the person himself who eliminates the South Node activity. With the South Node in Libra, it is the partner who does the changing.

Eventually, the nodes must be balanced, and with much effort they do get balances, but it is a constant vigilance. In the beginning, they are simply out of balance. The South Node is as a pot running over, while the North Node is as a pot half empty. When they are balanced, it is like a stereophonic sound; you hear both as one, for you are standing in the middle, giving due attention to both.

Interpreting the Nodes is really not complex; it is simply a question of putting the pieces together. This is fairly easy when delineating one chart. However, when we do comparisons between charts we have four pieces to work with in considering each of the Nodes. These must be interwoven into one. Quite a task, but it can be done.

The South Node area is not perfection, not quite. However, it can become so. It is the karmic area where we can, and must, give of ourselves, teach, and help others. It is where we have a wealth that needs release.

Another example of interpretation is South Node in Virgo in the third house. Here we have the Virgo perfection which is over-attention to detail, and possibly an over-critical nature. South Node in Virgo in the third house is a person with a keen mind. With other aspects giving it leverage, this is the lecturer, the technical writer, and possibly one who must learn the Pisces way of compassion and understanding. Since North Node in Pisces is in the ninth, he must learn enthusiasm, expansion, and optimism. The balance must come by rising above the over-detailed, over-critical tendencies.

Next, we have South Node in Pisces in the third. Think of what the house does, and what Pisces stands for and put them together. This would give a very dreamy nature, one given to writing poetry, and one with psychic tendencies—if aspects to Mercury correspond. With aspects of the Node to Mercury, it would accent greatly the psychic talent. This South Node person is able to express well his compassion and understanding for those within his environment.

Let us weigh the aspects to the nodes. First, we have a trine from the South Node to the Sun, and a sextile from the North Node to the Sun, or vice versa. This gives a successful ego, self-confidence, strong individuality, and ambition. With a trine from the South Node to the Sun, the person is capable of genius (other aspects not too diverse). This is a person long-lived, especially if the North Node is in the eighth. If the trine is from the North Node to the Sun, this success seems to come effortlessly. When the person has self-confidence, it is easy to adopt and establish a new area of learning. If this aspect of the North Node to the Sun is a sextile, then there will be grater than normal opportunity for growth, but not as easily obtained as with a trine.

Mars trine the North Node gives action and great energy lending itself to the nodal position's work. Mars square the nodes is sharp force and, like all squares, can overextend itself and "blow out." The square is an intense force and not easy to handle, but it can work if one is aware of it and its power.

Usually, squares between other planets in the chart, though

not touching the Nodes by aspect, must be corrected and disciplined before North Node development can begin. Squares always attract attention. If this square between two other planets touches and involves the nodes, the square must be corrected by the struggle and effort before lasting success can come form the nodes.

This correction takes effort, for it is easy to fall back to the security if the South Nose affairs when struggle for growth fails at times. Many times a North Node development is arrested or stopped altogether because of Victorian codes of ethics. To name a few examples: ninth house (religion), fifth house (love), and eighth house(sex).

If, in the comparison of charts involving close relationships, we find another who has his Sun in trine to our North Node, this is similar to our having the aspect ourselves. It gives a strong magnetic pull and is a strong indication this person can or will play a karmic role in our destiny. We grow and learn easily under this influence, for it gives us confidence in ourselves. Naturally we need to look at other aspects between the charts, but the Sun trine the nodes is a strong influence, not easily overruled. It builds ego, and we are less shy concerning the new growth at the North Node.

The South Node in aspect to the Moon seems to be part of the past. How, why, and where are speculations that need unraveling, and we need astrologers who can and will keep and open mind to find these answers. The position of the Moon, by sign and house falling on the other's chart, can give a clue as to where, when, and how this former relationship may have been. We have a few leads, and only by constant work and research can we begin to see a pattern. Everything seems to be interrelated; we only need find the key. The strongest clue of all is the very definite sensation that we have known this person before.

A trine from Mercury to the North Node in one chart, making a trine to the Sun in another's chart, gives a fabulous grand trine. This combination stimulates minds in both, with the confident ego of the Sun included. It is endless strength and opportunity. Other squared aspects touching it can only stimulate and promote it.

Now consider nodes squared in both charts. This can be good. Take the nodes in one chart of Aries and Libra, and in the other chart of Cancer and Capricorn. This is a cardinal grand square which means leadership. Rivalry is involved, but not necessarily consciously. We now are weighing the Nodes, nothing else. This can be a strong jab in the side, or a strong jerk of an arm. They confront each other with a push to move forward. It can be like being pushed into water and not knowing how to swim, so you sink or swim—and ninety percent of the time you swim. It isn't the effortless strength exerted by the trine between charts, nor is it always silent inspiration. But it can have its lighting, for it is a force that works.

A close conjunction between Saturn and South Node in two charts can indicate a strong duty felt between them, some kind of disciplinary action, or loss, or sacrifice. This is karmic with the square aspect bringing the loss. Under the law of karma, the loss helps balance the books. Neptune and Pluto in close aspect to the Nodes between charts also indicates karma, and this in relation to the nature of the planet and signs involved shows the nature of the karma.

Saturn in the North Node, along with other aspects between two charts, would influence the North Node person's growth, helping him feel a responsibility and duty in connection with it. The Saturn person is the taskmaster, the teacher, the person from whom the North Node certainly will learn a lesson. Even though there is an overflow at the South Node, the person still feels a lack in this area because of its Saturn influence. However, Saturn is asking only discipline and stricter use of the Mars force, which also influences the South Node.

Bernice Prill Grebner

Karma

In Sanskrit, karma means act, deed, or work. Whatever, it seems to be the point that indicates our destiny. This is especially true concerning the nodal axis, but Saturn also plays a major part in our karmic destiny. We were born during a certain cycle to fulfill a certain action, or certain karma. Call it what you will, the fact remains we are required to learn, to do, to compensate, to atone for a certain thing, and we can do that only during a certain period of time.

South Node Heritage

The South Node is the faculty learned form a long succession of reincarnations of the soul. Another explanation is that it represents the last of a long line of a certain heredity strain. It is an inherited faculty, for which we haven't had to struggle to achieve. One of the main purposes of our life is to control this gift instead of letting it overflow and control us. There is a danger of destroying the new growth at the North Node by too much concentration at the South Node area. We always need to be aware of maintaining a balance at the nodal axis.

Relationships

Keep in mind that the Moon is something we carry over from past lives. Is it that which we must control and rise above. This faculty and influence of the Moon is associated with the South Node and seems to be a place were we also must give; it is a point of release. When we try to get at the Moon by sign and house; we become emotionally defeated and up tight.

The sun by sign and position seems to be associated with new learning, the direction of the soul in growth. However, when this Sun is conjunct the South Node, this becomes a little complicated and needs individualized interpretation by a good astrologer, for other factors need to be taken into consideration. The Sun should be associated with the North node.

The depositors of the nodes seem to be points where balance can be attained; and as I have stated before, the nodes need to be balanced because they tend to become bottom-heavy. This is especially true when the Sun is conjunct the South Node. But then look to the depositor of the Sun. When interpreting the nodes (or any other part of the chart) consider these five questions: What is happening? Why is it happening? How is it happening? Where? When?

What are the South and North Nodes? Why are the aspects to the nodes? How are the signs of the nodes? Where are the house positions of Nodes and also of Sun and Moon? When are the progressions and transits to these points?

Remember, when the Sun is conjunct the South Node, or when it makes any kind of strong aspect to it, there exists a strong ego at this spot that has to be purged in some way, or be changed. This person seems to have been too egotistical in a past life.

South Node Through the Houses

First House (or South Node in Aries)
   South Node in the first is the egotist.
   This is the person who tries too hard and, as a result, comes on strong at first. It gives a strong pioneering spirit with a "me-first" attitude. There is an ability to do all things well by oneself. This position can give a changeable personality. He tries too hard to be a special personality. This person may think in terms of his physical body being superior to others. He has a tendency to push himself too hard because of a lack in partnerships. The problems in life seem to be very much concerned with self. He can be the fearless pioneer of new concepts or new activity.

Second House (or South Node in Taurus)
   South Node in the second is determination.
   This position gives the person a dissatisfaction with money earned, or with working conditions. It may give many changes in jobs, or more than one job at one time. The person is always seeking the ideal way of adding to his own resources. This also can lead to financial difficulties. South

Node here gives us one who enjoys the physical pleasures, but who needs to learn balance and control of appetites and senses by creating beauty for the world. Second house South Node can give an inability to earn completely one's own way. Satisfaction and success in this area usually is delayed. It can give the person stubborn pride but great loyalty to a cause or a person.

Third House (or South Node in Gemini)

South Node in the third is subjectivity.

The person has the ability to express himself very well, and is keenly interested in mental pursuits. This gives a strong psychic tie to brothers and sisters, and could bring loss of one through death or separation. It can give writing ability with favorable aspects to Mercury, Venus, or Neptune. There is a strong urge to share knowledge with others. South Node here denotes a duty in caring for brothers and sisters who may continually drain the individual. There is also much involvement in activities for the community. It is most difficult for the person with South Node in this position to finish his formal education. The person would rather read and study on his own, or he goes back to school in an on-again, off-again way. This is an influence that gives impatience. There could be many small accidents if this Node is badly aspected. Involvement with neighbors is a continual problem.

Fourth House (or South Node in Cancer)

South Node in the fourth is the introvert.

This position of the South Node gives a seeking after perfection, especially in domestic matters, and gives a great depth of soul. It can cause many changes of residence for the individual. There is great dissatisfaction in this area, with a constant desire for a Shangri-la. The person wants to live a quiet retired life in seclusion and peace. There exists a shyness about him, and he would like to retreat from the public. He probably will adopt a parental role by trying to hold people too closely. He is usually very talented at repairing things around the home. If a woman, she is usually a good cook.

Fifth House (or South Node in Leo)

South Node in the fifth is attached love.

It is too attached and self-loving. With South Node here, there is an almost constant interest in love; the giving and receiving, and its pleasures. This gives innate knowledge in the rearing of children although not always immediate success. This nodal position can bring loss of children with aspects to it showing the degree of the loss. It bestows many loves—loves that are always changing—and gives a knowledge of love beyond the ordinary. The lovers usually turn into friends. Personal affections prove dissatisfying because of a certain idealism. There is constant searching for love, romance, and pleasures. This position delays a permanent love relationship. Receiving love is denied, it seems, until enough is given. If South Node is in Libra in the fifth, others in his life leave the person because he expects too much. South Node in Aries indicates the person's own egotism destroys love through impatience. South Node in Taurus demands the person's own money be spent for children, love, and pleasures. South Node in Scorpio demands the partner's funds be spent on children, love, and pleasures. This position gives an individual creativity leading to genius when well aspected.

Sixth House (or South Node in Virgo)

South Node in the sixth is the critic or the worker.

Here the South Node gives an instinctive knowledge on health matters and a drive to learn more concerning this. It gives a desire to serve others and a constant changing of working conditions. There is great attention to detail with the ability to weed out. This individual knows how to work, and much more so when favorably aspected by Mars. It denotes mysterious illnesses, those difficult to diagnose. Neptune in the sixth also indicates mysterious illness. If there is a conjunction of Neptune and South Node in the sixth, or Neptune in the first house, this compounds and accents the problem. This person can become a hypochondriac and is always running to the doctor. Many doctors and nurses have South Node in the sixth. The tendency to be critical and to take everything apart is strong with South Node in this location and can be, to some extent, severe when considering the sign involved.

Seventh House (or South Node in Libra)

South Node in the seventh is self-abnegation.

There is danger here that the individual will tend to indulge in all kinds of relationships. His partnerships and unions can become so involved that he may lose his individuality in others. This gives the probability that the person will marry successfully later in life. There is always a secret fear of losing the marriage partner. It gives innate knowledge and talent of how to be a good partner. Along with this comes dissatisfaction because of the South Node person's overly idealistic image of a partner. Marriage in this ideal sense may be tried many times and many times denied. He is not rational where partnerships are concerned, especially when South Node is in the sign of Libra. South Node in Scorpio in the seventh is troubled with sexual idealism and/or the partner's financial status. The person is capable of counseling others despite his own personal problems, or more probably because of them.

Eighth House (or South Node in Scorpio)

South Node in the eighth is secretive.

There is an innate knowledge or extreme interest in sexual matters as a true regenerative force. It gives a natural talent for the occult arts. South Node in the eighth gives a desire to be supported by another, or the partner's money is extremely important to him. It gives a knowledge and talent for handling other people's money. This person needs to lose reliance on partner's finances. He is not afraid of the thought of death or dying. It gives an extreme hunger for knowledge of the hereafter, coupled with an innate wisdom of our connection with the cosmic forces. Death seems to play an important part as a rejuvenative force in his life. There is a preoccupation with his sexual knowledge and prowess. However, he is very considerate of his partner's satisfaction in sex. Both North and South Nodes in the eighth can bring fame after death, depending on aspects to the Sun and Moon.

Ninth House (or South Node in Sagittarius)

South Node in the ninth is objectivity.

This gives instinctive knowledge of philosophy, theology, and science. It gives an objective desire to study higher abstract truth. There may be many changes in religious thinking because of an inner need to seek the truth of our being. But on a lower scale this may result in a tendency to cross-examine. It promotes interest in the basic theories and concepts of religion, social ideas, and the metaphysical. The person should learn to study these subjects realistically with his intellect instead of daydreaming. South Node in the ninth, at its best, is a genius at separating fact from fancy, especially when favorably aspected to Mercury or Uranus. South Node in Sagittarius is very idealistic and outspoken, and has to guard against becoming overly optimistic. This position gives creative intelligence, aside from book knowledge. It also causes the person to think the grass is greener on the other side of the fence.

Tenth House (or South Node in Capricorn)

South Node in the tenth is the extrovert.

With this position there is great ability to deal with the public as the person easily understands its needs. This is similar to the Moon in the tenth, but coupled with the innate genius in public affairs. He does not take time to relate on a personal basis because of an inner need for public acclaim. It also can bring disappointment and dissatisfaction with regard to his vocation, bringing in many changes. If South Node is in Aquarius in the tenth, he can be a leader of unpopular causes. The South Node here gives a tendency to resist control by others. At its best, the power and success attained in the world must be used to assist others. When the person is able to do this, then destiny for this position will be met. At its worst, when used for vain self-glory, he fails. Here the uppermost thought should be control of selfish desires for ambition and power.

Eleventh House (or South Node in Aquarius)

South Node in the eleventh in unattached love.

It is too detached and selfless. Friendships, social affairs, reforming drives, advanced ideas in human relationships are part of the perfected South Node in the eleventh. This person is friendly, open, and instinctively knows society's needs. Friends can turn into lovers, and he truly needs an intense love affair to fulfill his soul's destiny. People with the South Node in the eleventh house suffer real discomfort in close relationships between members of the opposite sex. They have very utopian ideals where human needs are concerned. This varies with signs and aspects, but these ideals must be used as a basis of leadership in social and/or political causes where he can teach others humanitarian ideals. Here, we find many government officials or those dealing with the public welfare.

Twelfth House (or South Node in Pisces)

South Node in the twelfth is sensitivity.

Here is the person with a talent for working with the sick or mentally insecure. It gives a drive to seek seclusion and an inclination to meditate. With bad aspects it could give an alienation from society. This position seems to be karmic, and there is a very definite secret, sacrificial service of some kind involved, depending upon sign and aspects. The person with the South Node in the twelfth house may have a martyr complex, which must be used at its highest in sacrificial service and delving into the secrets of the subconscious, bringing them to the light of the conscious mind. This position gives many nurses and doctors.

The South Node has the influence of Mars conjunct Saturn. Too much of the Saturn accented can produce fear and hold the Mars action back; this can give poor timing. Mars represents energy; Saturn a cycle of time. With this combination we need to take stock of the issues involved and do something about them. The trick is to use this energy of Mars in the right amount by the disciplining of Saturn in an area of selfless service rather than over possessiveness.

North Node Through the Houses

First House (or North Node in Aries)

This person needs to learn to do things for himself, to rely on his own initiative. Life seems to force him constantly into situations where he will have to act under his own volition. He should develop a personality that the public identifies as being individual, and he needs to take a personal stand on things. North Node in the first is forced constantly to project himself, depending upon the sign position. The sign would indicate the reason for the projection of self. He will need to accomplish things through the power of his personality and to develop self-sufficiency.

Second House (or North Node in Taurus)

The person having this position will be faced with the problem of earning and managing his own resources. It is instinctive for him to depend upon others' finances and resources. He must build his own if his destiny is to be fulfilled. This nodal position needs to develop practicality, physical endurance, and perseverance. North Node here must relate loyalty to sex, and must bring it down to earth and reality.

Third House (or North Node in Gemini)

This position makes it difficult for the person to express his deepest feelings. This must be learned by constantly exchanging ideas and feelings with others. This must be forced before he can reap fulfillment. He needs to develop the ability to share his sensory awareness in his life with those in his social environment, and needs to receive from them their awareness and impressions. He needs to relate easily to his environment and to work for the betterment of that society. The key words are communication and subjectivity.

Fourth House (or North Node in Cancer)

With the North Node in the fourth there should be a development of the domestic life. He needs to learn the art of going into seclusion. He must be alone with himself at times to develop his own depth of soul, to dig deep and get to the very roots. Possibly, he would have to learn the role of nurturing, helping another grow, as in helping to sustain life. This person would need to establish a home, to care for it and learn what it takes to do this. There may be a problem in connection with a parent or an imbalance in his love for them—loving one more than the other—or it could give loss of one parent at an early age.

Fifth House (or North Node in Leo)

A person having this nodal position needs to learn to use his heart and become attached in a very personal way. He needs to love deeply and intensely on a one-on-one basis. There is also a deficiency or delay concerning children in his life. The children can be physical, mental, or spiritual offspring. He should develop a great desire to be creative in some endeavor. This person cannot seem to hold onto love until later in life because he simply does not know how. He seems able to succeed in this more successfully when he meets someone with South Node in the fifth. Aspects to the Node are very important in determining whether he has the strength to acquire this new growth. As an example, bad aspects to the Moon or Neptune could give emotional problems by losing touch with reality in this regard. North Node here needs to learn to consider self in loving. He may not be able to express his love fully.

Sixth House (or North Node in Virgo)

With this position he needs to learn to work and to be of service to others. He must learn to do for others with no regard for himself. He needs to lose the self-interest toward which he tends to gravitate. This also includes learning discrimination, attention to details, and discipline from too much daydreaming. He also must concentrate on health matters for the protection of his physical body. He needs to bring compassion down to the practical level.

Seventh House (or North Node in Libra)

This person has to overcome a tendency to work by himself. He needs to learn to work with a partner, to learn the balance it takes to do this. He has to strive for a close personal relationship with others. This relationship should bear some constructive fruit, whether business or marriage. This is quite a step because it leads to the death of the self-centered ego. The person then acquires the knack for becoming an arbitrator. He needs to develop an appreciation of beauty in the arts.

Eighth House (or North Node in Scorpio)

The North Node in this position forces the person to learn to accept another's financial help. Sometime in his life he will be forced to learn to accept the humility of taking from others. He also needs to learn the depth of experience in sex, its proper and beautiful purpose, and the regeneration and rejuvenation it brings to human beings. North Node badly aspected could cause either a breakdown or disturbing emotions when there is an imbalance in any of the eighth house activities.

Ninth House (or North Node in Sagittarius)

Many times when the North Node position in the ninth is not developed, it gives the person a tendency to defy the law in some way, or gives the inclination to find ways of working deviously within the law. This can indicate also a disregard for religion. The person may have a difficult time being ethical. Religion can be touched only subjectively. He needs to develop an interest in psychology, religion, and abstract philosophy. He must become more objective in his thinking and studying, expanding mentally and spiritually. The person with North Node in the ninth has to try to absorb and assimilate what is beyond his normal reach. He needs to become more objective in his interpretations within his immediate world.

Tenth House (or North Node in Capricorn)

A vocation should be followed, sometimes to the point of sacrificing home and domestic life. This means working for or with the public in some way. Through very sustained effort and great exertion, success in public life will be attained but requires personal sacrifice. The area of sacrifice can be ascertained by the aspects to this nodal position. When this Node is balanced finally with the South Node in the fourth, then the fulfillment of the great-person status will be obtained, and not before. This position, when followed, will give the urge to be a protector of great masses of people, to be a leader among them. Naturally, the influence of all of these nodal positions in the houses is dependent upon the signs involved. If the sign were Leo in the tenth, it would deal with children or some creative project, and the theater may possibly bring fame. One cannot read simply North Node in the tenth, but always must interpret the sign and aspects. If the aspects are trines and sextiles, the arrival at the North Node will come more easily, but if aspects are squares and oppositions, the arrival at the North Node may take more time and trouble.

Eleventh House (or North Node in Aquarius)

Much depends upon whether the sign involved with this Node is masculine or feminine, to denote the type of friends most favorable to the development of this house. This seems to be very important. People who have the same nodal axis—fifth and eleventh—by house and/or sign seem to understand each other better since they have the same direction to their destiny. Someone who has North Node in the eleventh will be helped greatly by someone with South Node in the eleventh. This person needs to learn the art of friendship and to become involved in some type of social endeavor or reform action. Here they must become as an Aquarian in the highest sense of the word: a true humanitarian. With this position there must be acquired the ability of true detachment and an independence in loving, for one cannot be dependent and be a true humanitarian. With the development of this North Node position comes a true strength and understanding of the human condition.

Twelfth House (or North Node in Pisces)

This position of the North Node takes self-sacrifice. It is helping those less fortunate, those handicapped or afflicted. This is done in a quiet, unassuming way. The person must learn compassion, learn to accept others as they are, and to help them in spite of any differences. This is the position of karma, and seems to call for some kind of payment. Many times this position produces doctors and nurses, and would seem to be an excellent way to fulfill this twelfth house Node. Since this is the house of the subconscious mind, the person needs to develop and release these vast resources, bringing them to the threshold of the conscious mind by expanding his ability to meditate. In its lighter vein, this is the sign of the poet, indicating another means of liberating the storehouse of the subconscious and its vast inspirations. The degree of success would depend upon its connection with Mercury, Jupiter, and the third and ninth houses.

For a finer, more pinpointed delineation of the Nodes by sign, you must consider the decante. The co-ruler of the decante would make a slight difference. For example, North Node in 18 Aries 12 would have the co-ruler of Leo, and would be considered a little differently than 24 Aries 10, which has a Sagittarius co-ruler.

Comments

If the house cusp sign is different from the sign the North Node is in, one would have to consider this sign also in the person's development and growth. For example, if Virgo is on the cusp of the eleventh, and the North Node is in Libra, Virgo and Libra both must be taken as lacking.

In the interpretation of the North Node, the person may be lacking only one particular facet of the description of the houses and signs. He nay not need to develop all the qualities described.

He may not be developed in all qualities at the South Node description, but may follow his genius in just one facet of qualities at the South Node.

North Node has the influence of Venus and Jupiter. It gives intense appreciation and respect for the area by the sign and house where the Node is located. There is popularity in this place with optimism and cheerfulness. This is a lucky place.

Each planet and sign has a positive and a negative side. Our own thinking can call on either side when transits and progressions tick off this planetary influence. Mercury would be very important by sign and aspect to the planets and Nodes. Mercury shows our personal thinking and our capacity to understand our new North Node growth. Without proper thinking we cannot progress very far.

Evolved souls differ from those not so evolved in that spiritually evolved people respond to the higher vibrations of the planets and the nodal development. Example: Uranus, originality rather than eccentricity; Mars, courage rather than recklessness; Taurus, willpower rather than stubbornness. Before interpreting the Nodes in a chart, look at the total chart to get an overall picture of the evolvement of the soul. It will make a difference in the analysis.

The South Node in any sign gives qualities to the person from that sign even though there may be no other planet in that sign. If another planet is in the same sign, it gives added emphasis and direction to the sign's placement.

Physical problems related to the South Node are: Aries, headaches, eye problems; Taurus, the throat; Gemini, respiratory system; Cancer, the stomach; Leo, the heart; Virgo, digestion problems; Libra, kidneys; Scorpio, reproductive organs; Sagittarius, muscular spasm; Capricorn, arthritis, skin problems; Aquarius, circulation; Pisces, feet or elusive illnesses.

One is given much energy to react to the things indicated by the sign and house at the South Node. Then, after he takes action, duty and responsibility set in. Transits over the planet ruling the sign of the South Node can help interpret where the responsibility and duty lie. This transit can indicate a new period in one's life. It gives a desire for power where this South Node is located.

North Node can give an affectionate and expansive nature where located. It gives the opportunity but, at first, extra effort is needed, and the person feels shy at the North Node area.

The Nodes are locked in when the North Node is located in the opposite sign's houses in the natural zodiac. Example: North Node in Cancer in the tenth house, or North Node in Aquarius in the fifth house. Destiny also seems locked in, and these people are held to balancing their Nodes more easily. Their outlook and outlet to life is much more singular. However, bad aspects to this nodal position can upset the apple cart. When a square to the Nodes is set off by transit or progression, this can cause attention and action at this squared position, taking away from the Nodes. But after much work and concentration on the affairs of the North Node, they suddenly seem to have equal power at last. The South Node never should be neglected in pursuit of the North Node; however, balance always should be maintained. When the Nodes are not locked in (e.g., North Node in Cancer in the eighth) there is another outlet for this nodal activity and energy. When North Node in Cancer is in the eighth, it also would include eighth house matters in the growth.

When the Node is within two degrees of the Ascendant, it gives an unusual type of personality and a very distinctive appearance.

Everything in the chart seems to dissolve eventually into the nodal axis. There seems to be a magnetic pull of some kind; that is, unless some very harsh bad aspects pull it another way. This is not the usual case.

If a person has South Node in the third house, consider first the qualities of that house. Consider the affairs of the third house and the qualities of the sign in which the South Node is located, then blend them together. The same is true for the North Node position. Consider the aspects; this shows how and when the development of the Nodes comes about.

Aspects to the Nodes

When the Nodes are squared by a planet, there seems to be a pull toward the planet's position by sign and house until the Nodes are balanced and set off.

Nodes Square Sun

This puts a stronger than usual accent on the Sun and its position. There is a greater awareness of the self or ego. It denotes the person who can be self-opinionated. However, this would cause an up-and-down belief in himself. There isn't the calm and poise that is found when a Node trines the Sun. This person is apt to be quarrelsome concerning things at the nodal positions. It is difficult for him to achieve success in life. There is difficulty in establishing balance of the functions at this nodal axis. The action and stress seem to come out at the Sun's position.

Nodes Trine, Sextile Sun

Success is assured when the affairs of the Nodes are blended favorably with the Sun's position. The person's ego is very good. He has proper motivation, above average intelligence, and is morally sound. This also gives great charm, good health, and long life, especially if North Node is in the eighth house. Constructive action comes naturally to successfully fulfill the destiny of the Nodes.

North Node Conjunct Sun

This gives a strong advantage to the North Node area. The ego and the new activity flow along the same path. Wherever the Sun is located is where there is strength, vitality, action, and warmth.

South Node Conjunct Sun

This gives greater difficulty in establishing the new growth at the North Node because the ego wants to stay at the opposite South Node area with the Sun. The ego feels better associating with South Node affairs; and in order to grow and learn, the person must buck a strong ego.

Nodes Square the Moon

This can give problems with health throughout most of the person's life. There is much emotional influence concerning the nodal area. There can be a passive intolerance of other's opinions. This aspect can cause some drastic change in the personality. It can exaggerate greatly the femininity of a woman, or can make the woman extremely coarse and rough unless well aspected by Venus. In a man it seems to make him less tender, less refined. Relations with the mother may be poor due to personality clashes. This person's personality can be misunderstood by others in first contact. For a man it may mean marriage, or unions with women of diverse age or social background, or marriage may be prevented or delayed. The action and stress seem to come out at the Moon's position and through problems with women. It causes inhibitions in expression and feelings which do not work to the best advantage of nodal balancing and growth. It is best to release the feelings some way.

Nodes Trine, Sextile Moon

This aspect gives a calm and steady emotional nature. In a man's chart it attracts a woman who will help him. It gives a cheerful temperament. The health is affected beneficially and the personality comes across well with the public.

South Node Conjunct Moon

This aspect is karmic in nature. This, as the square, can give passive intolerance of another's opinions. Part of the karma can concern home life or can be connected with the public, mother, or women in general. It gives a stronger development of the sign thus located.

North Node Conjunct Moon

This gives a pleasing physical beauty, especially if in an angular house. This person has a good personality, well received by the public. The feelings, emotions, and personality blend well with the North Node development and seem well suited for projection into the new area. In my opinion, Moon conjunct North Node makes it a more familiar territory than other aspects. This means the person has progressed further in his evolvement than a South Node conjunct Moon person. It favors a repeat life like South Node conjunct the Ascendant, or Moon conjunct Ascendant. For a man it can indicate help from women with his North Node area. For a woman it can mean great influence from her mother, or work with women on a personal basis or in an organizational way.

Nodes Square, Opposition Mercury

This may make the person suspicious, outspoken, and somewhat tyrannical. It may make the person seem aloof. Basically though, it gives shyness. This may be a clue to serious nervous problems if not handled properly. It is meant to increase the mental energies toward the balancing of the Nodes. There is a tendency to find fault and to exaggerate. Judgment can be poor, so the person may not be good at giving advice. This gives a fluctuation-type mind. When carried to its fullest and best, this exaggerated imagination can give success in the literary field.

Nodes Trine, Sextile, Conjunct Mercury

This is a good aspect for an astrologer, especially the trined North Node. It gives good spirits and a cheerful nature. There is a preference for young people. It gives an ability to write or lecture. It is fortunate for expressing the thoughts, as there is a clarity of ideas, especially with the trine or sextile. All aspects to Mercury have psychic value.

Nodes Square, Opposition Venus; South Node Conjunct Venus

This does not exactly favor happiness. This person is usually very sensitive and cannot express his affection comfortably. He cannot adapt easily to intimate relationships. For a man it may remove the woman he loves in some way, or may make the relationship difficult, especially if square. It may not deny love in his life, but it can put obstacles in the way that he must overcome. This diminishes the Venus charm and makes the feelings easily influenced. Venus square the Nodes tends to break up his numerous love affairs. Venus opposition the South Node designates an imbalance or excessive feelings. There can be great sacrifice to an ideal love. The square is not food for lasting love and may tend to make the person tyrannical and jealous. The Node square Venus is especially significant for it takes much of the person's attention. The interest goes to the sign and house in which Venus is located, and great force has to be exercised in balancing the whole T-cross.

Nodes Trine, Sextile Venus; North Node Conjunct Venus

The person with this aspect is affectionate and warm-hearted. He may tend to be very expressive and, with an aspect to Jupiter, to the point of being gushy. This adds to the Venus charm and makes for great popularity. This aspect in a man's chart makes him attract beautiful women with much charm of manner. This gives a nature that is dependable and well able to put action behind the feelings of affection.

Nodes Square, Opposition Mars

Along with this aspect comes cruelty or a stern nature. This person has sudden erratic bursts of enthusiasm and energy; he blows hot and cold. He usually wants to start new enterprises but loses interest in them when the first challenges are met. It gives impatience and may disturb the physical vitality which can cause physical suffering. It gives much sexual energy, sometimes to the point of sexual promiscuity. Squared energy (Mars) doesn't work well with the South Node area; it leads to excess. However, it does seem to work better with the North Node area where this excess is needed.

Nodes Trine, Sextile Mars

This aspect invigorates the sexual nature and gives much vitality. In a woman's chart, it gives her the magnetism to draw a vital man into her life. For a man's chart, it shows good sexual strength and strong vitality. It can give a feeling of independence because of the vital mature these people have. This person is well able to function physically in most things he attracts. He is able to undergo danger with great courage and has great endurance in conflict. It gives practical application of energy to the affairs of Mars and the South Node.

South Node Conjunct Mars

The South Node stimulates Mars passions and senses but can give poor timing, for the South Node influence pushes forward with passion and then pulls back. Action and fear need to be balanced. This is what the aspect is: action, then fear.

North Node Conjunct Mars

Mars energy is very forceful for North Node activity. This position over-stimulates and sometimes exaggerates sexual arousal. It definitely puts action behind the North Node growth.

Nodes Square, Opposition Jupiter

Here there is a lack of temperance; this person is at one extreme or another, never down the middle of the road. He can be overly religious or extravagant with possessions, and that can lead to catastrophe. He can be revolutionary and reckless. It gives great love of adventure, always seeking new experiences of some kind. Optimism is difficult to maintain at a steady level. It can give legal problems, especially in affairs of the Nodes. Example: third house, or Gemini, with brothers and sisters, people in the immediate environment.

Nodes Trine, Sextile, Conjunct Jupiter

This aspect indicates wholehearted pursuit of the nodal position's growth, and aids that growth in an effective way. It gives luck and good fortune in balancing the nodal axis. Few other aspects contain such potential as this one. There is enthusiastic endeavor, and one cannot beat this. This is also the philosopher, the lawyer, or the world traveler (the adventurer). This can also be the leader in a religious group.

Nodes Square, North Node Opposition, South Node Conjunct Saturn

Sacrifice or surrender are the key words here. Saturn's house position may cause neglect of the nodal position's growth, and the balancing of the nodal axis may be much delayed. Success is also harder to achieve where Saturn's position is located by sign and house. Wherever Saturn is located is where we feel a great lack; where a father's influence can be the most strict; where ambitions are thwarted. Other aspects taken into consideration, this is not a favorable position for a positive, enthusiastic spirit. Unless well aspected to Jupiter, the Saturn square must be corrected first by strict discipline in accepting responsibility that can't be refused. This position can give great loneliness. The life seems to be fated. Karmic conditions are indicated. Call it fate, karma, or what you will, it is that area which we can do little about except surrender to it in strict discipline. With this aspect, along with a good aspect to Jupiter, Jupiter's influence cannot be felt greatly until the discipline Saturn calls for is accomplished. The person who has this lacked discipline in a former lifetime; hence he is being forced into it in this life. The lessons of Saturn are patience, duty, loyalty, and being in tune and in step with time as it is. Their destiny is to get in step.

Nodes Trine, Sextile Saturn; North Node Conjunct Saturn

This can give considerable spiritual beauty and a great feeling of duty and responsibility. These people are in step. Here we have the ability to see the serious broad view and to stick to it. It gives considerable patience and fulfills the work of balancing the Nodes and learning an even greater lesson in this lifetime. It eventually brings luck and success due to the ability to make the required sacrifices. The conjunction of North Node to Saturn brings a Saturn opposition to the South Node. This is considerably easier to handle than the South Node conjunct Saturn opposition the North Node, for with Saturn working in opposition to the North Node growth, it takes considerably more effort to push forward. Without additional support in the chart it could be most difficult.

Nodes Square, North Node Opposition, South Node Conjunct Neptune

This person must be careful of drug and sex abuse, and over-stimulation of the imagination from overly idealistic thoughts. This power should be used for acting, singing, poetry, and understanding compassion. Some with this aspect seek false satisfaction in the senses. It gives a desire for seclusion and for impractical endeavors. As with all aspects, we must consider other aspects that can lessen or emphasize. Many times this aspect indicates two sides to the nature—a pull of undue idealism and being overly sensitive against power-hungry, selfish gratification. Badly aspected to Mercury, it can give mental imbalance in one degree or another. This position, when touched by transits and/or progressions, could bring confinement or hospitalization—forced confinement with the square; self-imposed isolation from the other aspects. The karma will be according to the nature of the sign and house position, and the nature of the aspects.

Nodes Trine, Sextile, North Node Conjunct Neptune

Here we have a generous, hospitable, sympathetic nature, ready to help all in need. This person is talented in music and the arts, or has a great appreciation of them. His sensitivity and awareness are very keen. It inclines him to metaphysical studies. He seeks the seemingly impossible. Since there is a high spiritual development, he easily gets help from others, either in this world or from the next. This is related to beauty and creativity and is said to be a gift. This seems to be a favorable karma. The person is favorably inclined to higher spiritual love. Another theory is that this person is from planet Neptune.

Nodes Square, Opposition Uranus

This person varies from moody and sensitive to reckless and defiant. He has a love of drastic action. He has a longing for authoritative power. The person with this aspect is eccentric, with fitful energy which limits him in making good use of his talents. It is not good for partnerships or marriage because it gives too great a desire for freedom. He wants unrestricted living. Other unfavorable aspects by Mars and Saturn can give suicidal tendencies or unknowing self-destructive ways. The square gives public attacks on the person's morals and honor. It can compel him to take risks, making him accident prone.

Nodes Trine, Sextile, Conjunct Uranus

This indicates an unconventional attitude with much respect for the value of being individualistic. He tends to the unusual. He is the adventurer and is romantically eccentric (somewhat like Venus trine Uranus). His mind is way ahead of the masses. He can express himself best through humanitarian and social reform, by being a living example. Look to the sign and house position to see how and what this social reform consists of.

Nodes Square, Opposition, Conjunct Pluto

This will give sex problems of some kind or problems concerning a partner's money. He seems forced to project himself into a separative action. This, all too often, seems to indicate a confrontation with death, or problems dealing with the occult.

Nodes Trine, Sextile Pluto

Even the good aspects to Pluto can be separative, but the separation is for the good of the nodal axis growth, and this can be interpreted by sign and house. It denotes force and depth. There can be great success in the occult and in delving into the mysteries of life after death. Here, too, is the person who has a great awareness of the rejuvenating power of sex; one who can deal with the beauty of sex in a positive way.

South Node Sextile, Trine, Conjunct Midheaven

This aspect gives the person changes of vocation, or disruptions of some kind concerning his dealings with the public.

North Node Sextile, Trine, Conjunct Midheaven

This aspect can give the person delays in starting a vocation until after the age of thirty. After the North Node is set off by progressions and/or transits, then he can become successful if favorably aspected.

North Node Square, Opposition Midheaven

This gives a sharp force for the action concerning the person's vocation and is good if he does not push it too far. If pushed too far, squares give danger of a blow out. The opposition takes away from the development of either position, for there is an imbalance that has to be corrected.

South Node Closely Conjunct Ascendant

This gives an unusual appearance to the body. The square or opposition to the Ascendant is bad for the health. There is, also, a negative aspect to the personality. South Node conjunct the Ascendant gives a very short or a very tall stature—seldom average.

South Node Closely Conjunct Any Planet

This gives an unusual trait to the nature of the planet touched. It brings out the unexpected.

North Node Closely Conjunct Ascendant

This gives a most pleasant, tall appearance resulting in an easy acceptance by the public. North Node lends itself more to the charms of Jupiter and Venus. Venus gives good looks, and Jupiter gives favorable form of body. It is especially good for a man's chart, for it makes him handsome. As he gets older he may tend to pick up weight, for the North Node can be generous. However South Node close to the Ascendant (within three degrees) gives an ambitious nature with more drive.

North Node Well Aspected to Any Angle

This is excellent for North Node growth.

As with any aspects in a horoscope, or between horoscopes, the closer they are to exactness, the more powerfully they will operate. This same rule applies to aspects between the Nodes and planets, Ascendant, or Midheaven. If the aspects are within three to four degrees of exactness, they will operate powerfully. If the orb of exactness is greater, the aspects will operate weakly.

Both North and South Node positions require great effort, with just as much attention at the South Node as to the North. We cannot lose the South Node development by putting too much effort in the North Node, for the Nodes must be balanced.

Why Failure at the South Node?

Each Node is in danger of changing or giving up the effort. At the North Node it is the person himself who is tempted to quit. At the South Node he seems to be more a victim of circumstances or conditions forcing him to change or terminate the action.

However, in each sign in which the South Node is located, the termination, change, failure, or separation, seems to be caused through the negative traits of the sign itself.

Examples of the reasons for these failures are as follows:

South Node in Aries—the change is caused by the person himself, or through some impulsive action of his own.

South Node in Taurus—the person's own selfish, stubborn, indulgent attitude.

South Node in Gemini—the shallow, fickle, variety-seeking nature

South Node in Cancer—too tenacious, too sensitive and overly emotional handling of the affairs

South Node in Leo—too domineering, egotistical, or overly dramatic

South Node in Virgo—too critical, petty, fussy, or overly discriminating

South Node in Libra—others cause the change, but Libra's inability to make up his mind contributes very much to the loss

South Node in Scorpio—excessive concentration on sex, possessiveness, overly secretive (thereby, not communicating), revenge-seeking nature, or misuse of other's possessions.

South Node in Sagittarius—desire for freedom, or promising things not given

South Node in Capricorn—being too unimaginative, autocratic, and overly cautious

South Node in Aquarius—too independent and tactless

South Node in Pisces—too impractical, submissive, and dependent

If any position in the chart is powerless through self-effort, it is the position of the South Node. However, great effort can direct it to the higher octave of the sign involved, thereby making it constructive instead of destructive.

The nodal positions Mars and Saturn seem to be stress points, where problems can and do arise. It is in these areas the person cannot easily handle the problems himself. This is when he consults an adviser (hopefully an astrologer!).

Nodal Dignities and Debilities

North Node is exalted in Gemini, ruler in Virgo, harmony in Libra, fallen in Sagittarius, detriment in Pisces, inharmony in Aries.

South Node is exalted in Sagittarius, ruler in Pisces, harmony in Aries, fallen in Gemini, detriment in Virgo, inharmony in Libra.

Gemini and Virgo are favorable to the North Node. Sagittarius and Pisces are favorable to the South Node. This is true also if the North Node is located in the third or sixth house. South Node is also more favorably placed in the ninth and twelfth house. Therefore, North Node in Sagittarius and Pisces is not as good and is much more difficult. South Node in Gemini and Virgo is additionally very difficult. Consideration must be given when North Node is in harmony in Libra and in inharmony in Aries. It is very wise to consider the dignities before giving a final interpretation of the Nodes in a chart.

Transits

Progressions and transiting planets affect the Nodes in relationship to their nature. Only the slower-moving planets seriously influence the Nodes. The faster-moving planets seem to have only a transitory effect. Progressions of planets aspecting the Nodes set off a new period in the person's life.

Transiting Mercury
Transiting Mercury brings love or inspiration from someone you love for North Node growth.

Transiting Venus
Transiting Venus could bring love or inspiration from someone you love for North Node growth.

Transiting Mars
Transiting Mars gives vitality and brings out action. The desire would be to do something.

Transiting Jupiter
Transiting Jupiter brings abundance, optimism, and luck. Religion could enter the consideration concerning the Nodes, or one may begin to be aware of a new philosophy relating to them. It also can relate to ideas that have to be expressed.

Transiting Saturn

Transiting Saturn asks discipline and duty of the nodal position. Possibly, considering the aspect made, sacrifice will be asked, or some condition with respect to the Nodes will be made permanent, or a lesson will be learned. Saturn transiting a conjunction of the North Node gives an influence of balance to the nodal axis, adding weight, since South Node has a Saturn influence. This calls for discipline and a duty-conscious experience to both North and South Node areas. Saturn's influence upon the Nodes is very important and has to do with the end or beginning of a karmic situation—timing.

Transiting Uranus

Transiting Uranus enlightens, separates, and tends to make one more individualistic and independent concerning affairs indicated. With higher evolved souls it can lead to cosmic awareness or consciousness. In any event it gives changed conditions in the person's life.

Transiting Neptune

Transiting Neptune, unfavorably aspected, may create sorrow, indecision, confusion. Favorable aspects will give more idealism, psychic awareness and/or highly spiritual sensitivity. Neptune is the spirit of sacrifice for something or someone that one loves more than oneself. Neptune also has something to do with divisions in cycles of karmic experiences in one's life.

Transiting Pluto

Transiting Pluto indicates a purging and a time of rejuvenation. It is where we seem forced or where we seem to ride roughshod over the affairs of these Nodes. It can be where we lose something or someone, especially when aspecting the South Node. We are coerced into clearing out and cleansing. Then take what is left and build again. The difference in reaction of transits and progressions would depend upon whether a trine, square, conjunction, or opposition is being considered. An example: Transiting Mars, when trined, is an easy energy, almost effortless, an incoming benefit. However, when squared, it is a sharp force, an extension of energy and action in a given direction.

Transiting Moon

Transiting Moon to the Nodes relates to them in a more short-term way. It can represent a distinct change in the life if this transit goes along with a progression. This is a monthly occurrence, so it is not a transit that is strongly powerful by itself.

Transiting Moon in the North Node can indicate a pleasurable experience with regard to the affections and emotions. It could indicate getting something new for the home, or it could indicate a pleasant experience with a woman in his life.

Transiting Moon to the South Node can be much more depressive, an unpleasant duty of some kind, or an extra amount of energy used in some way, perhaps in the home, or whatever. This depends upon whether the aspect we are dealing with here is favorable of unfavorable. If favorable it could bring about the long-awaited results in connection with the emotions—perhaps getting what you have earned. And, of course, all depends upon what else is being ticked off in the chart along with it.

Progressions

Ascendant favorably aspected to the North Node can bring strong attachments, sometimes marriage for a man, a general rise in life, and financial gain.

The Ascendant unfavorably aspected to the North Node can bring difficulties with attachments, or can cause extravagance or intemperance in habits.

The Ascendant favorably aspected to the South Node can bring marriage for a woman, birth of a child, great activity, gain through the acquisition of property.

The Ascendant unfavorably aspected to the South Node can bring poor health, liability to accidents, trouble with elderly people; the reputation or honor may suffer.

The Midheaven favorably aspected to the North Node may bring general rise in life, marriage for the man, vocational advancement, and influence through social affairs.

The Midheaven unfavorably aspected to the North Node can bring danger of lawsuit, loss though business affairs, jealousy, or loss though attachments.

The Midheaven favorably aspected to the South Node gives great activity of a worldly nature or vocational interests, possibility of acquiring a position of trust, marriage for a woman, or gain through an elderly person.

The Midheaven unfavorably aspected to the South Node

can bring disputes with others, difficulties in business, possible change of vocation, trouble with or loss of a parent, added responsibilities.

The Sun favorably aspected to the North Node can bring a prosperous time in a person's life. The self-confidence is good in connection with the North Node area. The health is also good. This aspect can be a real beginning in both the areas touched (a new cycle).

The Sun unfavorably aspected to the North Node can bring a period of poor judgment. This is a time when the person needs to reevaluate his path of destiny, or a change in the life is forced on the individual by outside conditions.

The Sun favorably aspected to the South Node can bring marriage in a woman's chart, a new responsibility in connection with an existing union, or a favorable change in the life style—or all three.

The Sun unfavorably aspected to the North Node can cause a separative action, or problems concerning marriage or unions, in a woman's chart. This aspect can be accident prone. It can affect also the vitality and strength of the individual.

An unfavorable aspect from the South Node to the Ascendant can bring a time of accidents and much abuse of the body through either working too hard or taxing your physical endurance in some way. It is also a time when there can be too much self accented—too much projection of that self. The best way to use this aspect is to take advantage of the influence the North Node can have in the seventh house of marriage and partnerships. This can be a favorable time for marriage and for building up relationships, but only if the right activity is used at the Ascendant. Remember, the South Node is stronger and there always has to be balance to gain the true lasting effect of this.

This is the reason I have read the South Node and the North Node placements separately, because, unless he has become very good at balancing this, he is feeling the effect of one over the other.

In this same connection, when the South Node is at the seventh, the North Node is at the first; they give a chance for self growth in a more favorable way. This can be an over-extension in emotion and effort where the partner is concerned, and the relationship is in danger of breaking. Always cool it where relationships of a deep union are concerned, for they can break at this time.

Favorable aspects of the transiting Nodes to the Midheaven can be advancement or an opportunity coming from the outside where vocation is concerned.

Unfavorable aspects to the fourth and tenth houses can bring problems in the home (fourth) or, if accented unfavorably, sickness of one or both parents. An unfavorable transit to the Midheaven can mean some danger of public scandal where you are concerned. This can indicate an attraction by your public to the deepest sensitive you.

A favorable transit of the North Node to the Midheaven could bring a very proud and happy feeling from your parents to you, for this is what you have earned in the way pride and respect from your parents. The progression of the nodes to the tenth and fourth would indicate your esteem going our to your parents.

An aspect to the fourth house from the Nodes, especially if there is a strong aspect from the Moon and Uranus, would indicate a move to another home. This same aspect to the tenth house, or to the Midheaven, would indicate a change of jobs, especially if this position was aspected by the rulers of the person's second and sixth houses.

Favorable aspects of the Sun and Moon to the Nodes are considered good karma, when something good can happen or when a person is in an earning position (getting paid). Unfavorable aspects of the Sun and Moon to the Nodes are thought to be bad karma, when something disruptive can happen or when you give or pay up. It is when the boomerang comes back to its source.

Progressions are ammunition; transits are the triggering agents. While the progressions are stronger in their influence and come from deep within our being, they do need to be triggered by a transiting planet (something happening from the outside). Progressions of planets to the Nodes time the cycles of a person's life; transits set off this action. The progressed angles, especially the Ascendant and Midheaven, can be very significant in setting off the purpose, not only of the Nodes, but the functions at the angles. It indicates a change of cycles and condition in life, giving a new direction. Transits are usually the experience; progressions are what it does to us, what it pulls out of our subconscious or potential.

A further comment needs to be made on the transits of the Nodes to the Ascendant and Midheaven, or to any angle of the chart. Transits, in my estimation, are only as effective as the use we make of the progressions in our charts. Transits cannot really affect us if we have not obtained true inner growth, which is what progressions are all about. Usually, though, a transit of the North Node to the Ascendant can make you feel good, happy with your world. It can be a time when you jump for joy and feel very enthusiastic about your world and how you appear to it. It can be a time for physical rejuvenation, or when your body is in a healthy period. When the Ascendant is in favorable aspect to the South Node, you have much vitality—almost too much vitality. You feel strongly physical. Why you feel this way depends upon the sign these Nodes are in. For instance, when the Ascendant is favorably aspected to the North Node, you feel enthusiastic about your world. The sign the Node is in will tell you why. Also, remember that when the accent is on the Ascendant, the opposite Node is affecting your seventh house cusp. When a transiting Node is affecting the Ascendant and the seventh house cusp, the only way this can remain in balance is if another planet is squaring this opposition or trining it, sextiling it, etc. This breaks the imbalance. Read this the same as the aspects from the planets to the Nodes.

An unfavorable aspect from the North Node to the Ascendant can bring extreme concern over clothes and appearance. It can cause extravagance with some kind of affection, whether this is another person or for an art object or something else.

The Moon favorably aspected to the North Node in a man's chart could bring marriage. The personality is well disposed to the North Node lessons. In other words, the personality makes it possible to attract experiences that gain him growth at the North Node area. The person feels well and is in good spirits. This is a favorable karmic influence. It seems to be a receiving time, when what we feel seems easier to handle.

The Moon favorably aspected to the South Node can give a person more calmness and courage, and brings harmony between feelings and discipline.

The Moon unfavorably aspected to the North Node brings suffering in love, or loss of a loved one. It is a time when the person will be giving more than he receives. It is when the emotional nature has to be taken to task.

The Moon unfavorably aspected to the South Node is a depressive time. It can bring problems and misunderstanding concerning women into a man's life. Both men and women can have disruptive conditions with home and mother (and a fickle public).

Venus in favorable aspect to the Nodes can bring pleasant affections and cultural interests. Income might increase.

Venus in unfavorable aspect to the Nodes can cause problems with the affections, and income might be disturbed. A man might lose a love or be depressed about lack of love from the woman in his life.

Mars in favorable aspect to the Nodes gives good vitality and inspiring arousal of the passions. Mars in favorable aspect to the North Node gives much drive and energy to activities at the North Node. This is true also to the South Node place. For a woman it can bring pleasant affections with the man in her life and good relations with him.

Mars in unfavorable aspect to the Nodes gives lowered vitality and energy not at its best; energy and vitality are out of balance. There could be also a problem with the passions. Sexual experience may get out of hand. This is more likely with a square to the Nodes—with Mars in the middle of this nodal opposition attracting attention and drawing to this overly abundant position of Mars. When Mars is opposing the South Node, it is conjuncting the North Node. This gives activity and growth because of the added energy factor at the

North Node, but the South Node has trouble relating at this time. Activities at the South Node area suffer and seem to tread water. Squares and oppositions to the South Node from Mars are quite different. The square to the Nodes from Mars, used at its best, can bring a tremendous balancing growth.

The rest of the progressed planets would be read the same as the transits. However, remember that the progressed aspects mean more inner growth, and the transits are a result of something coming from the outside. The only exception to this, I feel, is the progressed Sun on the Nodes, which can have the effect of both a progressed aspect and a transit.

Astronomical Explanation of the Nodes

The Moon circles the Earth each month, and as the Earth is moving around the Sun, the Moon must cross this orbit of the Earth twice in a month's time. At one time, to the north of it; at the other time to the south. The first crossing is called the North Node. The return is called the South Node. The Moon's Nodes always regress in motion, moving backward in the signs about three minutes each day. Wherever the Moon's latitude is at zero degrees, its longitude is the same as that of the Node, for it is crossing the ecliptic (the planet of the Earth's orbit). This complete revolution of the Nodes is accomplished in 18.6 years.

Other names for the Moon's North Node are the Dragon's Head or Caput, and it is represented by the symbol N. Other names for the Moon's South Node are the Dragon's Tail, or Cauda, and it is symbolized by n.

The normal tendency for the Nodes, as for the actual astronomical evaluation of their action, is to cause light to focalize at the North Node, and to cause light to scatter at the South Node. This is the influence it gives as it falls on the chart. The function at the South Node seems to spread its influence in the person's life to a great many people or events. It is where one gives. It seems to be where there is a karmic debt to pay. At the North Node there is a shyness, at first, and one seems depleted. It is where we learn to take in. Eventually, as the South Node proceeds with its teaching and giving, the necessary lesson is learned or the karma can be paid. Then success is met, and the process can be reversed and balanced. A person then begins to receive as he learns to singularize at the South Node, and to scatter or multiply at the North Node. In other words, when he learns the disciplinary influence that the Saturn-Mars connotation exerts over this South Node, he is meeting his destiny. By the same token, when he learns the growth at the North Node with the Jupiter-Venus influence exerted there, he begins to give at this point.

There is a strong indication that the Nodes must be balanced, and perhaps reversed, in the sense that the action at the South Node must become singularized, and scattered at the North Node. This cannot be stressed too much.

Nodal Points in the Charts of Famous People

Carl Jung

Carl Jung (July 26, 1875), the great psychologist-astrologer, had his North Node in Aries in the first house, and South Node in Libra in the seventh house. The North Node at 11 Aries 45 is trined by the Sun at 2 Leo 20, making a grand trine to his Midheaven at 11 Sagittarius. It is easy to interpret his success at striking out in his own and pioneering in a new direction. He succeeded in following his North Node in Aries.

Duke of Windsor

The Duke of Windsor (June 23, 1894) had North Node in Aries in the second house, with a square to his Sun at 2 Cancer 21. Here, again, there is a trine from the 4 Sagittarius Midheaven to North Node in Aries. He, too, struck out in his own and, with South Node in Libra, sacrificed much for marriage.

The Sun in Cancer in the fifth was most prominent in his life, for he gave up a considerable amount for love; the Duke gave up his British throne as Edward VIII for love and marriage to a commoner. He couldn't live without the woman he loved.

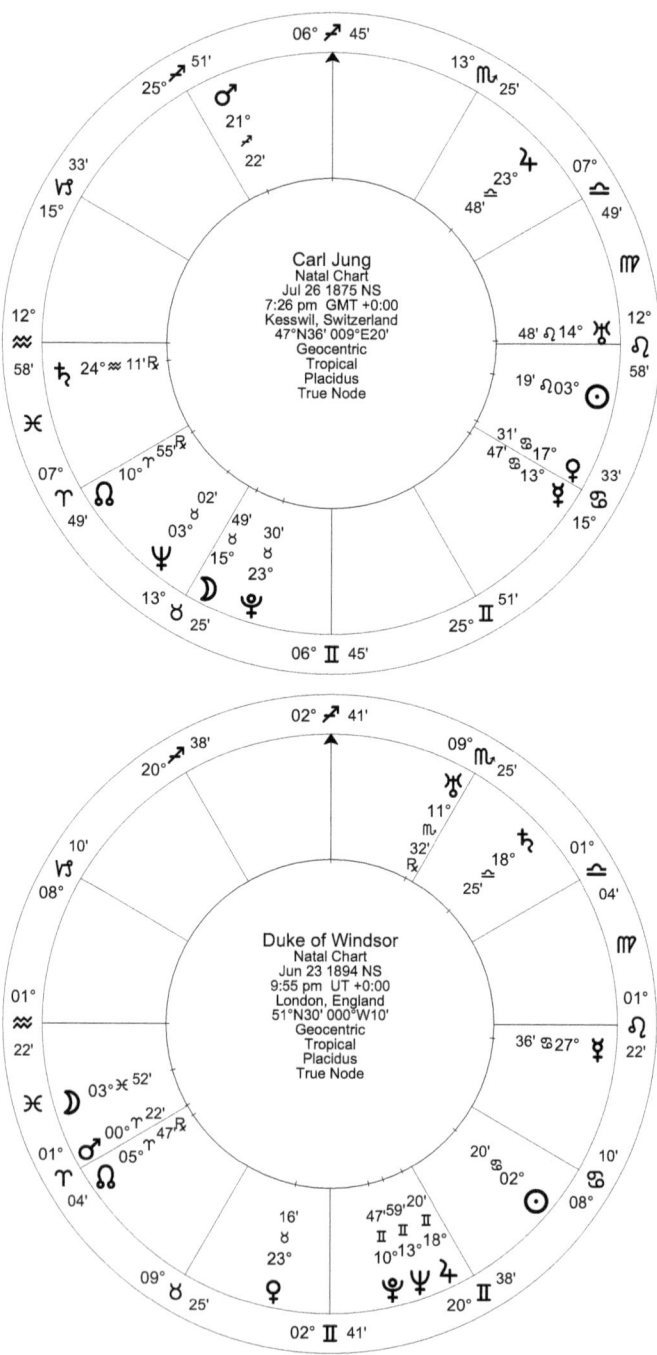

Herbert Hoover

North Node in Taurus in the twelfth occupies Herbert Hoover's chart (August 10, 1874). Since he acquired a great deal of money in his life, he seems to have followed his nodal pattern. Hoover spent much of his later years distributing resources. He worked extensively with the Marshall Plan in Europe after World War II (twelfth house).

Manuel Garcia

Manuel Garcia (January 18, 1866) was gored to death by a bull in Seville, Spain. He had South Node in Aries in the sixth house. This nodal axis was squared by Jupiter and Venus in his third house. His Moon was sextile his South Node, trine his North Node in Libra. He was a good showman, with Leo at Midheaven. His Nodes were also squared by Mars, which was in his second house. His chart seems to indicate too much emphasis on the South Node. North or South Node in the twelfth indicates a karmic destiny of service or sacrifice. Injuries or wounds (Mars) while earning a living (Mars in second) would be of a serious nature, reflecting adversely on health matters (sixth) and requiring hospitalization (twelfth). Injuries would change the cycle of his work and health (sixth, twelfth), as well as his income. The change of cycle would result in his overoptimistic thinking (Venus and Jupiter in the third). The significant influence seems to be South Node in Aries (Aries ruled by Mars).

Winston Churchill

Winston Churchill (November 10, 1871) had South Node in Libra in the first house, and North Node in Aries in the seventh. The South Node in Libra was conjunct Jupiter and Mars, sextile his Venus in the second. Opposing this first house South Node-Jupiter-Mars conjunction is the seventh house North Node conjunct Neptune. He did much to develop his South Node into genius. His Sun in the third house lent itself well to his North Node in Aries, and to leadership in war.

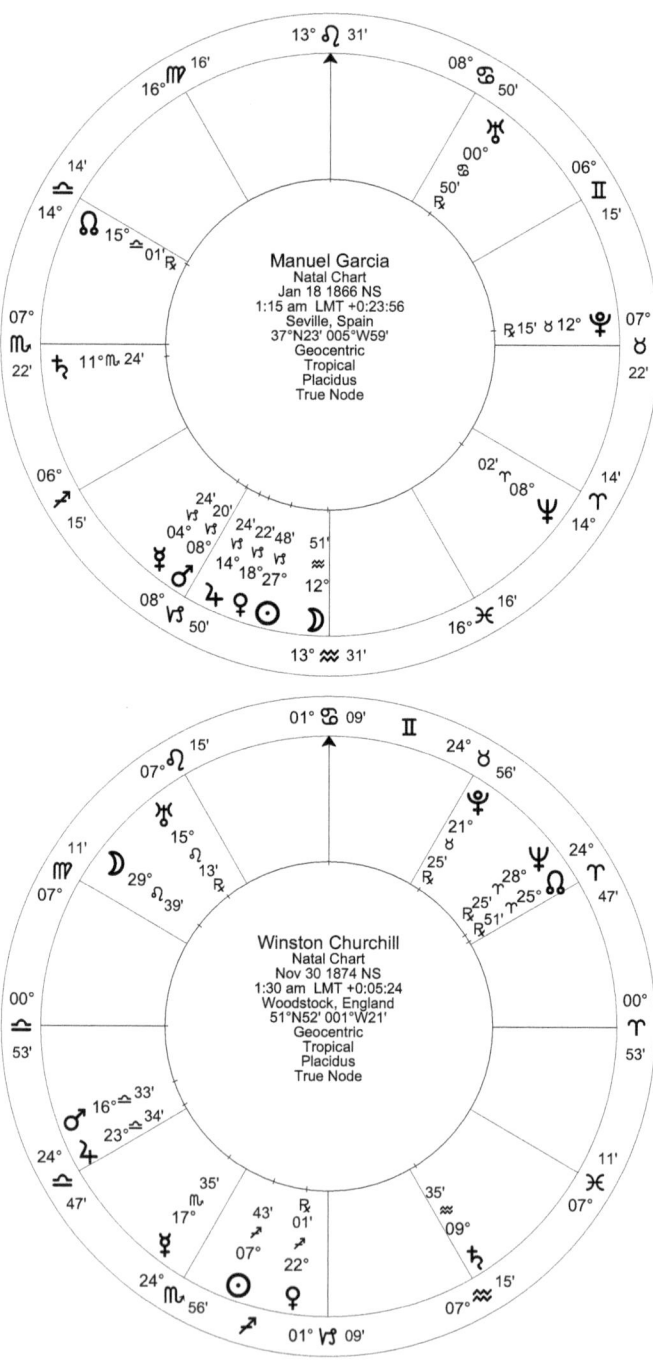

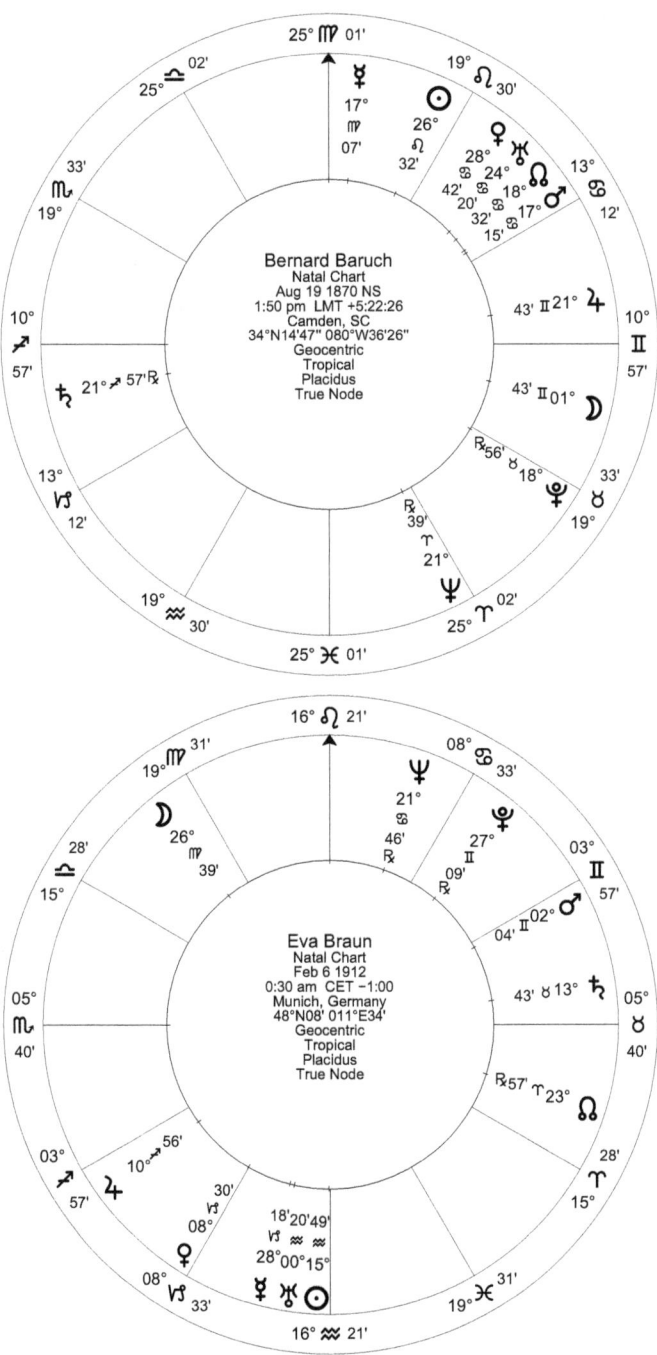

Pope John XXIII

Pope John XXIII (November 25, 1881) had North Node in Libra (which is in harmony with Libra) in the eleventh, and he certainly succeeded in bringing to the world social reform in religion. He was driven to improve the system and to give the world a more loving attitude in its relationship between religions. This pope sparked the ecumenical spirit between religions.

Bernard Baruch

Bernard Baruch (August 19, 1870) was a famous statesman and financier. He served as an unpaid advisor to every president from Woodrow Wilson to Dwight Eisenhower. In 1934, President Franklin Roosevelt appointed Baruch chairman of a committee to suggest legislation against wartime profiteering. After graduating from college, he had various jobs starting at three dollars a week. In the chart of Bernard Baruch, the South Node is in Capricorn in the second. He was a genius in handling other people's money as well as his own. His South Node at 17 Capricorn 09 was trine his Midheaven. The North Node sextiles it. The North Node was helped by a conjunction of Mars at 17 Cancer 15 (certainly giving him drive), and also Uranus. Taurus on the cusp of his sixth house contains Pluto within the house. This brings working conditions and eighth house affairs together, not to mention Taurus for money.

Eva Braun

Eva Braun (February 6, 1912), the mistress if the German dictator Adolf Hitler, had South Node in the marriage sign of Libra. The nodal system is squared by a ninth house Neptune and a third house Mercury. Hitler refused to marry Eva until allied bombs began landing on top of the underground hiding place where they were living. With the need to surrender to the allies coming closer, Hitler did marry Eva, but only with the condition that they both immediately commit suicide. Her suicide was accomplished through the use of poisonous drugs (Neptune). Her hopes for marriage, as well as her eventual marriage, were wiped out or dissolved (South Node in Libra) through circumstances over which she had no control (twelfth). The Mercury-Neptune opposition in square to the nodes encouraged self-delusion and false hopes. She was subjected to the paranoiac moods and desires of her partner (South Node Libra). She clung to her North Node in Aries in the sixth house. She should have learned to project herself in service to others. She should have developed self-reliance and discrimination in her associations. South Node in the twelfth is karmic and causes the person to retreat from the public, but squared by Mercury and Neptune (a self-indulgent, self-delusive influence) it is strongly karmic.

Synastry Aspects

Which aspect is influencing the two people in a comparison depends upon whether the person is accentuating the North or South Node in his life. The South Node is always the stronger in an aspect between charts; the North Node is always potential. In my estimation, they should be kept separate in your interpretation. If one person is paying more attention to the South Node position, this influence will be felt more strongly between them.

The North Node potential is always beneficial. Both influences are felt at times, depending on the strength of other aspects between them, but not necessarily both at the same time. They are separate influences and should be read as such. Example: Sun is opposed to the South Node, which means it is conjunct the North, but it does not mean both aspects are influential.

When the South Node in one chart is on a planet in another's chart, the power is with the South Node person.

Sun (in one chart) Conjunct South Node (in the other)

There is often an almost unexplainable attraction between two people having this aspect. Those who accept the philosophical concept of reincarnation explain this attraction as being karmic in nature, meaning that such people have had a close relationship in past lives with mutual problems still needing to be resolved. So they are attracted to one another again in order to work out the problems. There is often a feeling between such people that they already know one another; there is a strange sense of familiarity between them. The South Node person seems to have a stronger attraction to the Sun person than vice versa. The South Node often seems to drain the vitality and self-confidence of the Sun person. The destiny of the South Node person frequently interferes with the drives and needs of the Sun person. Resentment tends to build between them over the years, with the South Node clinging to the Sun person and weaving a web of dependency around the Sun. The Sun person may be flattered at first, but eventually seeks a way to free himself.

Sun Trine, Sextile South Node

For the Sun person this is a means of growth through the relationship. They need to establish a project together where growth can be accomplished. This may lead eventually to excellent constructive cooperation by both.

Sun Square, Opposition South Node

Here, there is a limitation for the Sun person in the area of the house and sign involved. There are disappointments and inner resentments by the one continually limited. The Node person begins a new cycle in the life of the Sun person.

Moon Sextile, Trine South Node

South Node in this position has a good effect in the Moon personality. It can strengthen domestic life, and the Moon easily responds. As with all aspects of the Nodes to the Moon, karmic conditions seem to exist, especially the South Node. The Moon person is held firmly by the South Node.

Moon Conjunct South Node

South Node can arouse easily the emotions of the Moon. It causes fluctuating conditions between two people. South Node has a tendency to be demanding if the Moon. Domestic changes may occur because of the contact.

Moon Square, Opposition South Node

This aspect puts strain in the personality of the Moon. The South Node person may discourage the Moon, and delays and hurt feelings always erupt. It connects to the past. South Node person forces changes in emotional response, the domestic area, and makes femininity seem more pronounced in both.

Mercury Conjunct South Node

Mercury becomes involved with serious thinking combined with the South Node's influence. The South Node person has something to teach Mercury. Mercury feels and responds to this discipline in mental pursuits. South Node seems to have greater power over Mercury. Mercury is forced to increase his knowledge. There can be a psychic attunement between minds, especially during times of crises.

Mercury Sextile, Trine South Node

Mercury appreciates knowledge and experience of South Node person, and is mentally stimulated. Mercury can bring out latent qualities in the South Node person. They both learn from this aspect.

Mercury Square, Opposition South Node

The key word with this aspect is criticize. The South Node person may underestimate the accomplishments of Mercury and may cause limitations and misunderstandings. This aspect can cause lack of tact in speech; however, used to advantage, it can challenge and spur Mercury to greater mental feats.

Mars Conjunct South Node

South Node can limit Mars' expression of personal desires, passions, and action. This aspect can cause rivalry, but it also increases the passion between the two. As a result, this could bring on sex problems. However, both of them come out of it more knowledgeable in the Mars (sex) area.

Mars Trine, Sextile South Node

The South Node person can truly said Mars. This aspect can bring unity of desire, and energy and action that is ambitious but cautious. It stimulates a disciplined energy.

Mars Square, Opposition South Node

The South Node in this comparison makes Mars less eager, less ambitious. South Node can push and frustrate Mars (that isn't all bad). Mars also can irritate and disturb South Node. This can cause conflicts or problems with the passions and sex. Nevertheless, it can be quite a sexual stimulant. Esoterically speaking, the people feel when they first meet that they have had a sexual relationship before. This can be true also of the conjunction.

Venus Conjunct, Trine, Sextile South Node

This can make South Node very intense in his reaction to Venus. There is much appeal to the emotions. South Node can be too possessive of Venus. There is a great feeling of responsibility to each other, for the affection is felt strongly as a duty.

Venus Square, Opposition South Node

This is a separative factor where love is concerned, and is also quarrelsome. It can have the same intensity as the favorable aspect, but can be more jealous. Love affairs can be very traumatic.

Jupiter Conjunct, Trine, Sextile South Node

This in a comparison between charts gives a material influence to both and an exaggerated tendency in each toward religion and philosophy. There is an overflowing of energy and inspiration in both that may be hard to handle. Jupiter does inspire South Node to pursue, with great interest, his South Node affairs and helps him give.

Jupiter Square, Opposition South Node

This aspect seems to be a reversal of the trine, and the

South Node person block Jupiter, puts obstacles in the way of his expansion. Jupiter will be frustrated and will feel confined. There may be disagreements in moral and religious issues. The South Node person can force the Jupiter person to express the meaning of Jupiter in the chart with a resulting change in his life.

Saturn Trine, Sextile South Node

This gives to both a stability and a drive to succeed. All Saturn-South Node contacts, including this trine, are karmic in nature. With this trine and sextile there exists a great sense of honor and responsibility for one another. As with the Saturn-South Node contacts, it gives the impression to both that one may have been a parent to the other in a previous existence.

Saturn Conjunct, Square, Opposition South Node

Saturn restricts and restrains, and sometimes completely blocks the South Node person's development in the area of South Node activities. South Node may put a strain on Saturn, and cause Saturn moods of depression, or may give great feelings of responsibility for South Node.

Uranus Sextile, Trine South Node

This is an excellent combination of Uranus' new ideas, creative ability and inventiveness with South Node's experience and development. Their common goal will be constructive. Uranus give South Node courage to bring out more talent and genius in his South Node area.

Uranus Conjunct, Square, Opposition South Node

With this aspect there may be friction. Uranus wants to rebel, South Node wants to hold, Uranus wants to break. Sign and house positions of Uranus and South Node determine the nature of the rebellion.

Neptune Conjunct, Trine, Sextile South Node

This combination gives a psychic tie. It is creative and causes more idealism in both. It is excellent for an interest in psychic phenomena, astrology, and the occult. It is bad if both tend to habitual indulgence in drugs or alcohol.

Neptune Square, Opposition South Node

This aspect between charts can lead to misunderstanding and deception. It can be emotionally disturbing and demoralizing.

Pluto Trine, Sextile South Node

There is a strengthening of will power in each, and it is excellent in working together on some research project.

Pluto Conjunct, Opposition, Square South Node

Problems arise in sexual experiences. This can encourage sexual perversion if one already is inclined that way. Other aspects giving strength, they may experience a desire to harm each other to one degree or another. The South Node person may be responsible for a feeling of isolation on the part of a Pluto person in the square aspect.

When the Nodes in two charts are in opposite signs and houses, they seem to be most understanding and helpful to each other. An example of this: one person has South Node in the fifth; the other South Node in the eleventh.

Sun Square, Opposition North Node

Sun person challenges Node person's growth. As a result Node person takes on more than he can handle. The Sun expects too much; hence crises and frustration.

Sun Trine, Conjunct, Sextile North Node

Here there is a loyalty, generosity, and a desire to bring out the best in each other. It creates a strong desire to help one another. This is a strong magnetic attraction, and an unselfish attitude toward one another. It gives the North Node person strength and vitality for growth from the Sun person. The Sun to North Node aspect between charts is destiny in the making. It adds to the spirituality in both, and to self-confidence of each.

Moon Conjunct, Trine, Sextile North Node
The domestic and feminine urges of the Moon harmonize well with the love and spiritual growth in the North node. There is a spirit of consideration for each other and a strong attraction between the sexes. The union between two people who have this aspect (especially the conjunction) seems destined. It is something connected with a past life that continues into a future life. It gives a great influence of domesticity between them. The Moon can teach North Node to appreciate the domestic circle, or in some way the Moon's nature will be absorbed by the North Node.

Moon Square, Opposition North Node
One person promises the other more than he can give, and this causes disappointment. They can demand too much from each other. There may be difference in social interests. This is very emotional and there is too much feeling.

Mercury Conjunct, Trine, Sextile North Node
An aspect of Mercury and North Node which stimulates intellectual pursuits and growth. There is mutual encouragement of talents, and appreciation of the intellect in each other. Mercury's reasoning power keeps North Node's ideals and visions reasonable, and North Node expands the Mercury person's educational pursuits.

Mercury Square, Opposition North Node
Mental interest will not blend in all instances. Each will accuse the other of having a petty mind. However, this can be good, for it may and can force each into new areas of intellectual endeavor, and has a far greater potential for extending mental areas for both if the power between then is used wisely. As in all squares, the power can be good, but there is risk of a blow out.

Venus Conjunct, Trine, Sextile North Node
Self-confidence and optimism are a result of this influence. Sometimes the conjunction gives extravagance in each other.

There is companionship and sympathy between them. Venus will encourage North Node and will show affectionate interest. This aspect is mutually beneficial.

Venus Square, Opposition North Node

There is a different attitude toward beauty and cultural things. They may not be sincere with each other regarding affections. This may cause and irritating effect and can bring about hurt feelings. However, it is not necessarily separative in itself; other aspects would have to do the actual separating.

Mars Conjunct, Trine, Sextile North Node

This gives energy to the North Node position. It brings a drive and push similar to this aspect in an individual chart. North Node is stimulated by Mars in the area of North Node activities. It creates ambition, vitality, and activity in both.

Mars Square, Opposition North Node

This may give rivalry between the two. Mars may drive the North Node person against his better judgment, or beyond his capacity. The Mars person may tend to be too impatient with the North Node in his new area of development, resulting in disputes between them.

Jupiter Conjunct, Trine, Sextile North Node

Optimism and self-confidence are enlarged here. The inspiration to develop along spiritual lines comes to both. There is generosity and tolerance toward each other. Jupiter expands North Node area's talent for growth.

Jupiter Square, Opposition North Node

This creates a difference of spiritual ideals, and this difference may cause misunderstanding. Jupiter may expect too much of the North Node person. There may be a lack of sincerity. However, this can be like the jerk of an arm and may move the North Node forward. And that is good.

Saturn Conjunct, Trine, Sextile North Node

Saturn brings discipline and responsibility to the North Node's development. Saturn can advise North Node very well. This aspect may increase the sense of duty between them.

Saturn Square, Opposition North Node

Saturn delays and puts obstacles in North Node's way. Saturn may criticize and restrict North Node, but may make some kind of sacrifice toward North Node's new growth, at best.

Uranus Conjunct, Trine, Sextile North Node

Uranus stimulates creativity in North Node. They will respect each other's need for freedom and individuality. There may be some kind of humanitarian project between them. It can be a stimulus for social good.

Uranus Square, Opposition North Node

Uranus will interrupt and change plans of the North Node. This aspect is not good for North Node's development; it can stimulate, but it can cause lack of responsibility. A strong Saturn aspect between them would have to exist before this aspect would prove to be non-separative.

Neptune Conjunct, Trine, Sextile North Node

This is a very idealistic and spiritual contact. There is a strong psychic tie that can be used for great constructive good in the area of love and compassion for others. Neptune will be able to bring out latent talent in the North Node. There is a karmic connection involved with this aspect.

Neptune Square, Opposition North Node

Neptune can mislead and deceive North Node. Neptune can be insincere and very impractical where North Node's growth is concerned. This is an overflowing aspect that can lead to overindulgence—a karmic debt.

Pluto Conjunct, Trine, Sextile North Node

This encourages character improvement in both and can be strongly occult (and mentally penetrating). It causes the persons involved to feel there is a strong bond between them—perhaps a bond that even death does not break.

Pluto Square, Opposition North Node

Pluto can be too demanding for the North Node to measure up. Pluto pulls and pushes and absorbs North Node. Pluto will frustrate the ideals and aspirations of the North Node person, possibly destroying incentive.

Synastry Interpretation

It is up to the astrologer to interpret which of the Nodes is felt more strongly in aspect between two people. Generally, one is influential, but both can be active between them. Wherever North Node isolated is where we must make an accurate commitment as to how we believe or how we are to behave, being true to ourselves. And we must accept the truth of the results.

The Ascendant of one chart in close conjunction with the Node of another is strongly physical, especially if the South Node is on the other's Ascendant. The North Node on the Ascendant is more inclined to make the Ascendant person feel important, optimistic, and expansive.

When the North Node of one person's chart falls in the seventh house of another's chart, the North Node will learn from this person. This can be important and lucky for partnerships and marriages.

If, for instance, the South Node falls in the seventh house of the same chart, the Seventh House person will be led by the strength of the South Node person. South Node exerts a powerful influence—not necessarily destined to last. It is destined to teach both a lesson from the experience. Wherever the nodal axis falls in the other's chart is where the area can get out of balance. The South Node does the teaching. Judgment will have to be made as to whether the Nodes are in aspect to each other before a final delineation can be made. Favorably aspected Nodes between charts can give lasting influence; unfavorably aspected Nodes can cause a separative action.

Moon conjunct North and South Nodes is a particularly strong magnetic attraction. Sun conjunct Nodes plays on their egos. Neptune on the Nodes gives an idealized relationship of some kind. Saturn conjunct and square the Nodes creates discipline, brings sacrifice between them, or could be devitalizing. Jupiter square the South Node test spirituality of the two. Venus trine South Node gives a tendency to over emotionalism and over solicitation between them. Venus square South Node gives disturbing reactions, or the attraction may not be felt by both. It can cause unfaithfulness by one and jealousy in the other.

Comparison Between Charts of Nodal Axis

Cardinal—Means leadership, and rivalry is involved. It can, however, be as strong jab in the side. They confront each other with a push to move forward. It can be like being pushed into water, so ninety percent of the time you swim. It can have its lightening, but it is a force that works.

Example: South Node in Aries square South in Capricorn; North Node in Libra square North in Cancer.

Mutable—Can bring on conflicts with Virgo's criticism. It may lack action and force because each may adapt too quickly to circumstances, preferring to take the easy way out. They do not move forward in growth as a result. It can work better if Sagittarius squares Pisces; if Virgo and Gemini are in square rather than Pisces square Gemini or Virgo square Sagittarius.

Fixed—Conflict between a generous humanitarian nature in one and a materialistic, emotional drive in the other. Both are very stubborn and fixed, so there can be a stalemate in the push forward, each blocking the other's progress.

Example: South Node in Taurus square Aquarius; North Node in Scorpio square Leo North Node.

One must consider not only a comparison of houses and

signs, but house and sign together. For example, North Node in Virgo in one chart on South Node in the Sixth in the other chart. This can lead to a balance between them, the same way as a comparison of South Node in the sixth and North Node in the sixth.

In a comparison of charts, when one person's North Node falls in the other's tenth house, it can improve growth in that house's affairs through inspiration and stimulation of the tenth house person.

When one person's Nodes are aspected favorably to another person's Nodes by trine or sextile, they are fortunate together for this nodal growth. The blending flows along smoothly without strife.

They can make or break each other via the aspects they have to each other's Nodes. Take the example of one who has a badly aspected Node by square from Mars or Saturn. If this badly aspected Node is aspected favorably by the other person's Nodes by trine, whether to the Nodes and/or to Mars and Saturn, the person's bad effect from Mars and Saturn is lessened by the influence of the relationship to the other person. Naturally, it also may go the other way; if there is a bad aspect from one person's Nodes to the other person's Nodes, it would be a harsh or combative, and even separative, influence. I am speaking now mostly of squares. However, squares can be either good or bad, depending upon how we use this energy. Most of the time this squared influence form another person's Nodes is disruptive, but it can cause greater growth much faster than the trines if it can be handled. Much depends upon how fan each person has evolved—whether they respond to the higher influence of the squared aspect between them.

The conjunction of the Nodes is not as good for growth between people, because they are too much alike in this particular growth pattern. It can be worked out if other aspects between charts to the Nodes show growth.

Conclusion

Time is very diffusive. All of us here within this cosmic structure are bound by it and are projected into space. We are taken forward into motion whether we will it or not. Not being able to make time stand still, our task remains to learn to flow with it. To do otherwise is to expend our life force in a futile attempt to fight the current in the stream of life, a current leading us to a higher plane of growth. Our resistance weakens the positive thrust forward.

Each individual must follow his own particular pattern set forth at the second of his birth. Each has his own map of what he has accomplished and what is yet to be done. It is the job of the astrologer to help people read these road signs of life. As the good in a chart is always dominant, the bad is recessive. Therefore, as astrologers, our positive approach to reading a chart is an emphasis on growth.

After coming into the temporal world of human life, we learn to grow and to enlarge our scope. We learn by flowing like the current of water in a stream, which is a positive God-given force. When we exert a force against the current, we get wiped out, because we are not as strong as the current. It is our endeavor, as people alike but different, to discover our roles in this molecular system, using time and its cycles to the fullest. This can be done by not fighting time or the natural structure of things.

With appreciation to all my associates and friends, living and dead, I give thanks for the inspiration and work I could not have accomplished by myself.

Appendix 1
Nodal Theories

Many brilliant and learned astrologers researching in the field of Lunar Nodes and other areas of astrology have gone before me and prepared the way. Many will come after me and have! Without their original foresight, my own research and original discoveries could not have been possible. I commend these brilliant thinkers. Astrological awareness is in a constant state of evolvement and perfecting. This can never be done by any one astrologer, but the many of us working together will obtain the total picture someday. We are, in reality, all working toward this similar goal—although some may not think so. He who thinks he is working alone is deluded. We, as astrologers and research people, should constantly keep this in mind. Newer and better insights keep coming.

All theories have a degree of plausibility. It depends upon your level of evolvement and awareness what you espouse and how you respond. Keep that in mind; let your mind be open to all theories. No one theory is more true than another. All fit somewhere in the big puzzle of astrology and cosmic awareness. It would be a bit like playing God to make a statement that this or that theory is definitely correct and this or that theory is definitely wrong.

Astrology is alive and growing rapidly. We, who seem to be in the thick of it, are fortunate. Please do not be deluded in thinking he who has been in it longer or he who has studied longer always knows best. Maybe not; some who come along are naturals. It is necessary for them only to reawaken their soul development from another time, or perhaps they have direct contact with the Uranian ray of wisdom. Please also understand that naturals are not common. On the other side of the picture, do not be a "Johnny-come-lately," thinking you know it all after only a short period of study. He who is genuine in his wisdom of astrology will be the first to admit he or she still has much more to learn—even if he or she has already been at it for 20, 30, 40 years. By their humility shall you know them.

The aspects to the Nodes are only as important and influential as you are evolved in awareness of them. There are different levels of awareness to which we respond. We can respond to the aspects to the Nodes as we have that awareness.

It depends upon whether you are responding to the physical, mental or spiritual dimensions. Perhaps the karma of the South Node is not so much a physical payment as a mental and spiritual giving.

The South Node does seem to show karma; the North Node does not. The differences of opinion among the experts on this subject are merely differences in levels of awareness or consciousness. All truths are useable. It depends upon your level.

Appendix 2
Current Transiting Nodes and their Effects Upon Society

South Node in Aries—obviously gives a preoccupation with self and self-interests. We were supposed to grow in relating to a mate, but did we? You, the reader, are the only one who can answer that for yourself. Mars rules South Node in Aries, which seems to have influenced us by putting a great accent on the physical represented by sexual, energetic dancing and music, among other things.

South Node in Pisces—there may be a need to sacrifice for the common good and to begin to work and serve each other. Helath concerns may become more of the natural methods. Music will begin to change and become more inspirational and emotional. Perhaps romance will become more poetic and dancing may involve closer body contact.

South Node in Aquarius—will bring the true brotherhood of man into being. The real humanitarian endeavors can begin, not just be stimulated. However, the independence of the Aquarian influence may appear among the people. By this I mean that each person may begin to have the courage to be truly himself in the manner of expression.

South Node in Capricorn—it will influence in the area of responsiblity and discipline. There may be greater accents on concentration and fortitude. In this era the father may again be king. Perhaps, too, small business will again dominate the scene. And so on through the signs.

Appendix 3
Lunar Nodal Return for the Individual

This return is approximately every eighteen years and can be fulfillment or completion of a cycle. The opposition at nine years is a frustrating time but can also be the beginning of awareness from others and the need to see the other side. It is also a time at the opposition when we realize our lessons can be learned and eventually fulfilled.

The square of the transiting Nodes to the natal Nodes is a time for action that may be initiated by problems. This can let the person see a different way of arriving at the destined growth and does not have to be considered as negative in any way.

The Lunar Node return cycle seems to indicate a stage where decisions are forced upon us with a mew and still greater nodal development being possible.

Each time the progressed Moon makes an aspect to the natal Nodes, this sets off a new cycle in the nodal development. No growth need be final. Even where a certain development or perfection seems to have taken place, it can become even greater. The person can become a saint or a genius with great illumination. All is possible, depending upon the determination of the individual soul.

For example: South Node position in the eleventh may show a development or interest in friendship but at a new cycle; it can be released to an even higher level where the self can gain a development as a great humanitarian by becoming interested in some special cause for all the people.

Appendix 4
Additional Thoughts on the Nodes

God, or the Force (call it what you will) teaches us easily, or we learn our lessons the hard way through experience at the North Node (depending upon aspects to it as to how).

House positions show the kind of experiences we will encounter; whereby we grow at the sign of the North Node. Eventually the experiences at the North Node get easier and will be accepted much more without effort.

For example: North Node Libra eleventh house. Lack of success in marriage, or a satisfying deep relationship can cause the person to use friends as crutches, or eventually true friendship will help the person understand deep relationships and true marriage.

The sign of the South Node is talent and experience by sign and house. Both go hand in hand are like hand in a glove. The sign is the hand and the house is the glove. Both become as one and cannot be separated.

The sign the Node is in represents the psychological need either fully developed (South Node) or to be newly developed

(North Node). The house it is in represents either the familiar or effortless experiences (South Node) or those experiences needed to develop the North node's psychological needs as described by house position.

The Moon and its house seem to work with the South Node because the Moon represents the past. The Sun and its house work with the North Node because the Sun represents the new growth. The negative sides of both seem to be manifested or made apparent at the Ascendant. If the Nodes aspect the Ascendant, this is much more potent and active.

The ruling planet of the South Node and its house location indicate a karmic condition connected with the South Node (or where a complete release to the cosmic influence is required). This is where the person seems to hold on, but also where he needs to release to a higher power before he can achieve the balance necessary in relationship to the axis of the Nodes.

The ruling planet of the North Node sign and its house position indicate an influence or experience that will expand the chances to achieve the new learning or growth.

Planets in the same house as the South Node are conditions brought over from the past and, depending upon aspects to these planets, what esoteric development was achieved, or it can show a picture of a past life (whatever you believe the past life of the soul to be).

Planets in the same house as the North Node and its aspects show new conditions, events, and destinies in connection with the growth of the soul.

I do not believe the South Node is a weakness—a familiarity, yes! It is a magnet that hold and (in that sense it is negative and feminine) can stop or retard us to give and project.

The North Node is electric, positive, and masculine by its nature. Therefore, it is natural for us to want to give our at the North Node—in our early development. Life forces us to take in at the North Node. We begin finally to realize we are balancing the Nodes when we absorb at the North Node and release at the South Node.

Life holds us to the North Node sign's development eventually and gives experiences and strength by the house position to do so.

If the South Node is trined by Saturn and Mars, it shows strong development and perfection from the past. Any other planet in turn aspecting this Mars and Saturn shows further definitions of the past. The sextile to the North Node by Saturn and Mars shows opportunities developing out of past talents and being utilized for the North Node.

If Jupiter or Venus is conjunct North Node there is a strong impetus to grow and expand the North node nature. A square to the Nodes from any planet gives much action and many varied problems and crises in the growth, depending upon the nature of the planet squaring them. The action quite naturally can cause slight changes in the direction although the ultimate destiny itself doesn't change.

South Node can bring experiences and people into your life that seem familiar which gives you a sense of repetition in some way. South Node by sign and house is instinctive so when anything goes wrong at the new North Node growth the person flops back to the place of the South node where he is comfortable. The North Node experiences have to be activated with effort.

South Node in the fifth of a child may give one parent with Venus retrograde or a Venus that went retrograde at the time of conception or birth.

South Node in the fifth or Leo gives a strong sense of loss of love which may or may not be reality. They try harder to love but never feel they are getting enough. They know and are sure of the love they give but cannot know about what they are getting in love.

North Node in Leo or North Node in the fifth house gives a strong sense of receiving love although it is the very thing they must learn to give on an intense one to one basis. They are not sure of the love they give. It sounds like a paradox, but it isn't. Test this theory for yourself.

North Node in Leo or the fifth must fight the obstacles or take off the mask to the loved one, because the loved one may be disguised to them in some way. For example, different ethnic backgrounds, differences in age or race, vast differences in looks (one may be handsome, the other not at all handsome or beautiful in the physical sense).

South Node in Leo or the fifth cannot understand why another doesn't love them automatically just because they themselves love the other so much and because they are willing to give so much extra love to the other. They cannot conceive of love being returned and it hurts them deeply when it is not returned. They simply cannot tune in on how much love comes back to them. Although deep in the back of their subconscious they feel love may leave them or take off to another. It is anther seemingly paradoxical situation but it really isn't. In some cases this South Node person may not be able to tell the difference between loving himself and loving the other. They are one and the same to the South Node in Leo or South Node in the fifth house person.

It is a question of the South Node person being influenced by a rulership of this Node like a combination of Mars-Saturn. Responsibility and sometimes a feeling of lack influence the person and give the necessity and drive of doing things and taking some type of action.

The North Node is influenced by a combination like Venus-Jupiter which gives optimism and receptivity.

Only when you have mastered the path of the North Node can you expect to receive at the South Node. Remember, at the South Node there is a projection or going out. At the North Node we have a receiving or coming in. This is the reason it is foreign to those at the South Node to be sure of receiving or at the North Node sign to be sure of giving.

South Node in Aquarius loves others platonically but may not believe he himself can give possessive love; therefore, sometimes he subconsciously resists an intense relationship where another tried to love him deeply. He may do things for others without their knowing it. He may not know who he is in relationship to those he loves because he may not love himself enough. He may not recognize love when it comes to him. When South Node in Leo gives something or does something for a loved one, you know it.

South Node in Leo needs only one true love; South Node in Aquarius needs many to satisfy in order to make up for a deficiency of not feeling enough love for himself or knowing what love on an intense basis really is. However, life forces the South Node in Leo person to experience many loves (in order to give)and the South Node in Aquarius to come to one true love.

South Node in the sixth house, if harshly aspected by the Moon, Mars, and Saturn can show a serious illness and possibly restriction because of it in a past life and into this life (to be overcome).

Appendix 5
Past Lives or Vocations Taking Little Effort

South Node Aries—Soldiers, adventurers, early American pioneers, mining engineers, government employees (especially aspecting Uranus), workers using tools (especially aspecting Mars), tradesman, policemen, firemen.

South Node Taurus—Farmers, artists, musicians or signers (especially aspecting Venus or the Sun), designers, jewelers, servants (especially aspecting Moon in Virgo in the sixth house), sculptors, clothiers, confectionery store owners (especially aspecting Saturn and Pluto).

South Node Gemini—Writers, school teachers, accountants, traveling salespersons, lecturers, printers, bookstore managers,(especially of aspecting Mercury and Jupiter), linguists (especially aspecting Jupiter).

South Node Cancer—Social workers, sailors, fishermen (especially aspecting Neptune), homemakers or realtors (especially aspecting the Moon).

South Node Leo—Athletes (especially aspecting Mars), brokers or bankers (especially aspecting Pluto), actors (especially aspecting Sun), governesses (especially aspecting Moon), gamblers (especially to a square to Jupiter).

South Node Virgo—Librarians, statisticians, psychiatrist (especially aspecting Pluto), scientists or inventors (especially aspecting Jupiter and Uranus), nurses (especially aspecting Neptune and Moon), thieves (especially a square to Mercury and Jupiter), keepers of small animals as in a zoo (especially aspecting Moon and Mercury).

South Node Libra—Diplomats (especially if aspecting Jupiter and Saturn), artists, architectural draftsmen, judges, decorators (especially if aspecting the Moon and Venus), counselors.

South Node Scorpio—Surgeons (especially if aspecting Mars, Uranus, and Pluto), investigators, detectives, chemists, undertakers, doctors or healers (especially if aspecting Pluto), revolutionaries (especially if in the sixth house), martyrs in a cause for humanity (especially if in the eleventh house and aspected by both Pluto and Saturn by square).

South Node Sagittarius—Lawyers, philosophers (especially if also aspecting Jupiter and Uranus), ministers (especially if aspecting Neptune and Jupiter), promoters (especially if aspecting the Sun and Pluto).

South Node Capricorn—Business executives (especially favorably aspecting Saturn), organizers, builders, public servants and (if favorably aspecting Uranus) high public officials.

South Node Aquarius—Explorers (especially aspecting Mars and Jupiter), aviators, astrologers (especially if aspecting Uranus and Mercury), electricians, psychologists, radio experts (especially if aspecting Uranus, Jupiter, Mercury).

South Node Pisces—Saints (especially if aspecting by trine to Moon, Neptune, Jupiter, Saturn), poets, workers in hospitals or films, psychics, clairvoyants (especially aspecting Neptune, Pluto and Mercury).

Appendix 6
Needs for Release

Some emphasis at the South Node needs to be released in order to attain the balance needed to be more aware of the North Node.

South Node Aries—They do things on the spur of the moment. They need to learn to plan further ahead and to do a little more weighing and balancing (North Node Libra). They may require at some time in their lives to be thrust alone or dependent upon self in order to learn the lesson of Libra by relating to others, realizing how much others really mean to them in order to learn the final release of self will.

South Node Taurus—Need to release materialistic values and to out them to practical good use in area outside of self.

South Node Gemini—Need to release subjective view of a more personal mature in order to accept a broader, more objective view. They need to travel farther spiritually and mentally and to be sure they understand everything they hear and learn.

South Node Cancer—Seem to require the release of all unnecessary money and possessions. There is the need to release the tenacious influence in order to learn the lesson of

Capricorn; thereby attaining balance between the family and a certain shyness with the public and a certain outgoingness. The key words are unnecessary possessions.

South Node Leo—Need to give love unconditionally, release psychological need to receive and the desire to dominate with love.

South Node Virgo—Need to release talent for perfection and discrimination, making room for compassion and understanding of other's weaknesses and to teach others how to serve.

South Node Libra—Need to release dependency upon a partner and to develop their own self-efficiency and ideas. They need to force independence and need to make a clear-cut decision and stick to it.

South Node Scorpio—Need to release strong desires and a strong drive to possess either an object, a person, or money, and the desire to destroy if necessary in the attempt.

South Node Sagittarius—Need to release the tendency to be too objective and need to let people get closer to them.

South Node Capricorn—Seem to require the release from so much concentration and the need to develop more sensitivity to their emotions and to acquire a home where they can learn the domestic necessities of life.

South Node Aquarius—Need to release the tendency to be too independent and platonic and to become more dependent upon an intense love and its expressions. They need to dare to need and to admit it.

South Node Pisces—Need to release the tendency to be too tolerant and to develop a need to be more discriminating in attitudes and actions. They need to be more precise.

Appendix 7
Examples

South Node Aquarius vs. South Node Leo

1. The big difference is one believes you have to love others first before you feel a real love of self.

2. The other feels you must love self first and be satisfied with self before you can ever love others.

Which is which? 1 is South Node in Aquarius; 2 is South Node in Leo.

Synastry

For example, South Node Aries relates to someone else's North Node in the first house. The South Node person will give experiences to this North Node person in order that the North Node person may grow. It is not easy but in their relationship they do grow.

Compare the sign and house comparisons between two people in this way: the North Node sign and the South Node house position of the other person and vice versa. Do this with any sign.

The South Node person gives the lessons and experiences. The North Node person receives them. It is the other way around with this same couple. An example of this is: one person has South Node in Libra's house and the other person has North Node in Libra. The same couple has one person having South Node in Aries and the other having North node in Aries house. In this way they give and take and each comes away from the relationship learning and feeling they have received something.

Appendix 8
Location of North and South Nodes

Year	From	To	North Node	South Node
1875	Jan. 1	Dec. 31	Aries	Libra
1876	Jan. 1	March 3	Aries	Libra
	March 4	Dec. 31	Pisces	Virgo
1877	Jan. 1	Sept. 21	Pisces	Virgo
	Sept. 22	Dec. 31	Aquarius	Leo
1878	Jan. 1	Dec. 31	Aquarius	Leo
1879	Jan. 1	April 11	Aquarius	Leo
	April 12	Dec. 31	Capricorn	Cancer
1880	Jan. 1	Oct. 28	Capricorn	Cancer
	Oct. 29	Dec. 31	Sagittarius	Gemini
1881	Jan. 1	Dec. 31	Sagittarius	Gemini
1882	Jan. 1	May 17	Sagittarius	Gemini
	May 18	Dec. 31	Scorpio	Taurus
1883	Jan. 1	Dec. 5	Scorpio	Taurus
	Dec. 6	Dec. 31	Libra	Aries
1884	Jan. 1	Dec. 31	Libra	Aries
1885	Jan. 1	June 23	Libra	Aries
	June 24	Dec. 31	Virgo	Pisces
1886	Jan. 1	Dec. 31	Virgo	Pisces
1887	Jan. 1	Jan. 11	Virgo	Pisces

Year	From	To	North Node	South Node
	Jan. 12	Dec. 31	Leo	Aquarius
1888	Jan. 1	July 30	Leo	Aquarius
	July 31	Dec. 31	Cancer	Capricorn
1889	Jan. 1	Dec. 31	Cancer	Capricorn
1890	Jan. 1	Feb. 17	Cancer	Capricorn
	Feb. 18	Dec. 31	Gemini	Sagittarius
1891	Jan. 1	Sept. 7	Gemini	Sagittarius
	Sept. 8	Dec. 31	Taurus	Scorpio
1892	Jan. 1	Dec. 31	Taurus	Scorpio
1893	Jan. 1	March 26	Taurus	Scorpio
	March 27	Dec. 31	Aries	Libra
1894	Jan. 1	Oct. 13	Aries	Libra
	Oct. 14	Dec. 31	Pisces	Virgo
1895	Jan. 1	Dec. 31	Pisces	Virgo
1896	Jan. 1	May 2	Pisces	Virgo
	May 3	Dec. 31	Aquarius	Leo
1897	Jan. 1	Nov. 19	Aquarius	Leo
	Nov. 20	Dec. 31	Capricorn	Cancer
1898	Jan. 1	Dec. 31	Capricorn	Cancer
1899	Jan. 1	June 9	Capricorn	Cancer
	June 10	Dec. 31	Sagittarius	Gemini
1900	Jan. 1	Dec. 28	Sagittarius	Gemini
	Dec. 29	Dec. 31	Scorpio	Taurus
1901	Jan. 1	Dec. 31	Scorpio	Taurus
1902	Jan. 1	July 17	Scorpio	Taurus
	July 18	Dec. 31	Libra	Aries
1903	Jan. 1	Dec. 31	Libra	Aries
1904	Jan. 1	Feb. 4	Libra	Aries
	Feb. 5	Dec. 31	Virgo	Pisces
1905	Jan. 1	Aug. 23	Virgo	Pisces
	Aug. 24	Dec. 31	Leo	Aquarius
1906	Jan. 1	Dec. 31	Leo	Aquarius
1907	Jan. 1	March 13	Leo	Aquarius
	March 14	Dec. 31	Cancer	Capricorn
1908	Jan. 1	Sept. 29	Cancer	Capricorn
	Sept. 30	Dec. 31	Gemini	Sagittarius
1909	Jan. 1	Dec. 31	Gemini	Sagittarius
1910	Jan. 1	April 18	Gemini	Sagittarius
	April 19	Dec. 31	Taurus	Scorpio
1911	Jan. 1	Nov. 6	Taurus	Scorpio
	Nov. 7	Dec. 31	Aries	Libra
1912	Jan. 1	Dec. 31	Aries	Libra
1913	Jan. 1	May 26	Aries	Libra
	May 27	Dec. 31	Pisces	Virgo
1914	Jan. 1	Dec. 13	Pisces	Virgo

Year	From	To	North Node	South Node
	Dec. 14	Dec. 31	Aquarius	Leo
1915	Jan. 1	Dec. 31	Aquarius	Leo
1916	Jan. 1	July 2	Aquarius	Leo
	July 3	Dec. 31	Capricorn	Cancer
1917	Jan. 1	Dec. 31	Capricorn	Cancer
1918	Jan. 1	Jan. 19	Capricorn	Cancer
	Jan. 20	Dec. 31	Sagittarius	Gemini
1919	Jan. 1	Aug. 9	Sagittarius	Gemini
	Aug. 10	Dec. 31	Scorpio	Taurus
1920	Jan. 1	Dec. 31	Scorpio	Taurus
1921	Jan. 1	Feb. 25	Scorpio	Taurus
	Feb. 26	Dec. 31	Libra	Aries
1922	Jan. 1	Sept. 15	Libra	Aries
	Sept. 16	Dec. 31	Virgo	Pisces
1923	Jan. 1	Dec. 31	Virgo	Pisces
1924	Jan. 1	April 4	Virgo	Pisces
	April 4	Dec. 31	Leo	Aquarius
1925	Jan. 1	Oct. 22	Leo	Aquarius
	Oct. 23	Dec. 31	Cancer	Capricorn
1926	Jan. 1	Dec. 31	Cancer	Capricorn
1927	Jan. 1	May 11	Cancer	Capricorn
	May 12	Dec. 31	Gemini	Sagittarius
1928	Jan. 1	Nov. 28	Gemini	Sagittarius
	Nov. 29	Dec. 31	Taurus	Scorpio
1929	Jan. 1	Dec. 31	Taurus	Scorpio
1930	Jan. 1	June 17	Taurus	Scorpio
	June 18	Dec. 31	Aries	Libra
1931	Jan. 1	Dec. 31	Aries	Libra
1932	Jan. 1	Jan. 6	Aries	Libra
	Jan. 6	Dec. 31	Pisces	Virgo
1933	Jan. 1	July 25	Pisces	Virgo
	July 26	Dec. 31	Aquarius	Leo
1934	Jan. 1	Dec. 31	Aquarius	Leo
1935	Jan. 1	Feb. 12	Aquarius	Leo
	Feb. 12	Dec. 31	Capricorn	Cancer
1936	Jan. 1	Aug. 31	Capricorn	Cancer
	Sept. 1	Dec. 31	Sagittarius	Gemini
1937	Jan. 1	Dec. 31	Sagittarius	Gemini
1938	Jan. 1	March 21	Sagittarius	Gemini
	March 21	Dec. 31	Scorpio	Taurus
1939	Jan. 1	Oct. 8	Scorpio	Taurus
	Oct. 9	Dec. 31	Libra	Aries
1940	Jan. 1	Dec. 31	Libra	Aries
1941	Jan. 1	April 27	Libra	Aries
	April 27	Dec. 31	Virgo	Pisces

Year	From	To	North Node	South Node
1942	Jan. 1	Nov. 14	Virgo	Pisces
	Nov. 15	Dec. 31	Leo	Aquarius
1943	Jan. 1	Dec. 31	Leo	Aquarius
1944	Jan. 1	June 3	Leo	Aquarius
	June 4	Dec. 31	Cancer	Capricorn
1945	Jan. 1	Dec. 22	Cancer	Capricorn
	Dec. 22	Dec. 31	Gemini	Sagittarius
1946	Jan. 1	Dec. 31	Gemini	Sagittarius
1947	Jan. 1	July 11	Gemini	Sagittarius
	July 12	Dec. 31	Taurus	Scorpio
1948	Jan. 1	Dec. 31	Taurus	Scorpio
1949	Jan. 1	Jan. 28	Taurus	Scorpio
	Jan. 28	Dec. 31	Aries	Libra
1950	Jan. 1	Aug. 17	Aries	Libra
	Aug. 18	Dec. 31	Pisces	Virgo
1951	Jan. 1	Dec. 31	Pisces	Virgo
1952	Jan. 1	Jan. 5	Pisces	Virgo
	Jan. 6	Dec. 31	Aquarius	Leo
1953	Jan. 1	Sept. 23	Aquarius	Leo
	Sept. 24	Dec. 31	Capricorn	Cancer
1954	Jan. 1	Dec. 31	Capricorn	Cancer
1955	Jan. 1	April 13	Capricorn	Cancer
	April 13	Dec. 31	Sagittarius	Gemini
1956	Jan. 1	Oct. 30	Sagittarius	Gemini
	Oct. 31	Dec. 31	Scorpio	Taurus
1957	Jan. 1	Dec. 31	Scorpio	Taurus
1958	Jan. 1	May 19	Scorpio	Taurus
	May 20	Dec. 31	Libra	Aries
1959	Jan. 1	Dec. 7	Libra	Aries
	Dec. 8	Dec. 31	Virgo	Pisces
1960	Jan. 1	Dec. 31	Virgo	Pisces
1961	Jan. 1	June 26	Virgo	Pisces
	June 27	Dec. 31	Aquarius	Leo
1962	Jan. 1	Dec. 31	Aquarius	Leo
1963	Jan. 1	Jan. 13	Aquarius	Leo
	Jan. 14	Dec. 31	Cancer	Capricorn
1964	Jan. 1	Aug. 2	Cancer	Capricorn
	Aug. 3	Dec. 31	Gemini	Sagittarius
1965	Jan. 1	Dec. 31	Gemini	Sagittarius
1966	Jan. 1	Feb. 19	Gemini	Sagittarius
	Feb. 20	Dec. 31	Taurus	Scorpio
1967	Jan. 1	Sept. 9	Taurus	Scorpio
	Sept. 10	Dec. 31	Aries	Libra
1968	Jan. 1	Dec. 31	Aries	Libra
1969	Jan. 1	March 28	Aries	Libra

Year	From	To	North Node	South Node
	March 29	Dec. 31	Pisces	Virgo
1970	Jan. 1	Oct. 16	Pisces	Virgo
	Oct. 17	Dec. 31	Aquarius	Leo
1971	Jan. 1	Dec. 31	Aquarius	Leo
1972	Jan. 1	May 4	Aquarius	Leo
	May 5	Dec. 31	Capricorn	Cancer
1973	Jan. 1	Nov. 22	Capricorn	Cancer
	Nov. 23	Dec. 31	Sagittarius	Gemini
1974	Jan. 1	Dec. 31	Sagittarius	Gemini
1975	Jan. 1	June 11	Sagittarius	Gemini
	June 12	Dec. 31	Scorpio	Taurus
1976	Jan. 1	Dec. 29	Scorpio	Taurus
	Dec. 30	Dec. 31	Libra	Aries
1977	Jan. 1	Dec. 31	Libra	Aries
1978	Jan. 1	July 19	Libra	Aries
	July 19	Dec. 31	Virgo	Pisces
1979	Jan. 1	Dec. 31	Virgo	Pisces
1980	Jan. 1	Feb. 5	Virgo	Pisces
	Feb. 6	Dec. 31	Leo	Aquarius
1981	Jan.	Aug.	Leo	Aquarius
	Sept.	Dec.	Cancer	Capricorn
1982	Jan.	Dec.	Cancer	Capricorn
1983	Jan.	Mid-March	Cancer	Capricorn
	Mid-March	Dec.	Gemini	Sagittarius
1984	Jan.	Sept.	Gemini	Sagittarius
	Oct.	Dec.	Taurus	Scorpio
1985	Jan.	Dec.	Taurus	Scorpio
1986	Jan.	Mid-April	Taurus	Scorpio
	Mid-April	Dec.	Aries	Libra
1987	Jan.	Oct.	Aries	Libra
	Nov.	Dec.	Pisces	Virgo
1988	Jan.	Dec.	Pisces	Virgo
1989	Jan.	May	Pisces	Virgo
	June	Dec.	Aquarius	Leo
1990	Jan.	Mid-Dec.	Aquarius	Leo
	Mid-Dec.	Dec. 31	Capricorn	Cancer
1991	Jan.	Dec.	Capricorn	Cancer
1992	Jan.	June	Capricorn	Cancer
	July	Dec.	Sagittarius	Gemini
1993	Jan.	Dec.	Sagittarius	Gemini
1994	Jan.	Jan. 31	Sagittarius	Gemini
	Feb.	Dec. 31	Scorpio	Taurus
1995	Jan.	Mid-Aug.	Scorpio	Taurus
	Mid-Aug.	Dec.	Libra	Aries
1996	Jan.	Dec.	Libra	Aries

Year	From	To	North Node	South Node
1997	Jan.	Feb.	Libra	Aries
	March	Dec.	Virgo	Pisces
1998	Jan.	Mid-Oct.	Virgo	Pisces
	Mid-Oct.	Dec.	Leo	Aquarius
1999	Jan.	Dec.	Leo	Aquarius
2000	Jan.	April	Leo	Aquarius
	May	Dec.	Cancer	Capricorn
2001	Jan.	Dec.	Cancer	Capricorn
2002	Jan.	Dec.	Cancer	Capricorn
2003	Jan. 1	April 12	Cancer	Capricorn
	April 13	Dec. 31	Gemini	Sagittarius
2004	Jan. 1	Dec. 25	Gemini	Sagittarius
	Dec. 26	Dec. 31	Taurus	Scorpio
2005	Jan.	Dec.	Taurus	Scorpio
2006	Jan. 1	June 21	Taurus	Scorpio
	June 22	Dec. 31	Aries	Libra
2007	Jan. 1	Dec. 14	Aries	Libra
	Dec. 15	Dec. 31	Pisces	Virgo
2008	Jan.	Dec.	Pisces	Virgo
2009	Jan. 1	Aug. 20	Pisces	Virgo
	Aug. 21	Dec. 31	Aquarius	Leo
2010	Jan.	Dec.	Aquarius	Leo
2011	Jan. 1	March 2	Aquarius	Leo
	March 3	Dec. 31	Capricorn	Cancer
2012	Jan. 1	Aug. 28	Capricorn	Cancer
	Aug. 29	Dec. 31	Sagittarius	Gemini
2013	Jan.	Dec.	Sagittarius	Gemini
2014	Jan. 1	Feb. 17	Sagittarius	Gemini
	Feb. 18	Dec. 31	Scorpio	Taurus
2015	Jan. 1	Nov. 10	Scorpio	Taurus
	Nov. 11	Dec. 31	Libra	Aries
2016	Jan.	Dec.	Libra	Aries
2017	Jan. 1	May 8	Libra	Aries
	May 9	Dec. 31	Virgo	Pisces
2018	Jan. 1	Nov. 5	Virgo	Pisces
	Nov. 6	Dec. 31	Leo	Aquarius
2019	Jan.	Dec.	Leo	Aquarius
2020	Jan. 1	May 3	Leo	Aquarius
	May 4	Dec. 31	Cancer	Capricorn

Appendix 9
Newer Information on the Lunar Nodes

There is a development at the South Node naturally, that has been established through many studies in the subject, but it is a development to the degree the aspects to the South Node say it is. For example:

South Node in Aries trine Jupiter would be a higher development than South Node Aries square Jupiter. A high development with South Node would be shown by good aspects in all ways to this Node. Naturally, there are very few pure influences.

What if there are not aspects to the Nodes? (This would be unusual but it can happen.) Have you ever known anyone like this? I have at one time and in that sense the Nodes did not seem to apply at all. (However, one example cannot be considered an absolute on the idea.)

Let us consider the other aspects of the Nodes to various planets.

Opposition, square Sun—self opinionated, ego problem, lack of self confidence displayed outwardly by an exaggerated ego problem.

Opposition, square Mercury—communication is the problem, also nervous problems develop or problems with a relative are not easily resolved.

Opposition, square Moon—emotions or domestic conflicts, difficulties with mother or health.

Opposition, square Venus—difficulties with love, cannot adapt, numerous loves easily ending in separations.

Opposition, square Mars—erratic bursts of temper, in some ways gives sexual promiscuity, impatience.

Opposition, square Jupiter—lack of judgment and temperance, religious or legal problems, or over extravagance.

Opposition, square Saturn—success and responsibility are hard to achieve. Discipline as a lesson, in its true light, is difficult. Problems with authority or the father.

Opposition, square Uranus—reckless, defiant, eccentric, unpredictable.

Opposition, square Neptune—self pity, possible drug usage, delusion with self and others.

Opposition, square Pluto—always separating self from others, hard to know, self destruction or its opposite, a rebirth.

These aspects are to the Lunar Nodes and involve an influence in nodal development and may not hinder other parts of the chart. An example of what I mean would be the Saturn lack of discipline—discipline may be achieved in other areas but not the Nodes.

Lack of achievement at the South Node is caused in many cases by poor timing—not exactly being on the beam. Some other force is pulling the person off course, and this force is pulling the South Node talent off course is usually a harsh aspect from one of the planets. This means the South Node development is not pure but has some distortion. When the South Node becomes more pure, when a major effect is made to develop it even more, then the person can rise to a higher development touching the true God Spirit of the sign.

Overall, if any stress points exist at the South Node it is the Mars and Saturn points in the charts that should be observed and watched. This is because Mars and Saturn rule the South

Node. If Mars and Saturn favorably aspect the South Node there is constructive action rather than fear and poor timing. A South Node point poorly aspected by Saturn gives a feeling of life being handled badly (which is mostly the person's own image rather than a fact). A poor Saturn aspect gives a tendency for the person to not face duties and/or practical reality. So the person's poor image causes the series of difficult experiences creating a treadmill influence.

There has been much written about the Lunar Nodes, but we cannot isolate their descriptions totally. Naturally, we go by aspects from the planets to the South Node, but the core of the problem, positive or negative, is Mars and Saturn. If the person has good aspects from north the North and South Node to Mars ad Saturn (or none at all) his/her chances of being constructive and coming to a higher, more cosmic level of development are greater. Also, the ability to advance and accept the new learning at the North Node is greater; hence balancing the Nodes. If the person has poor aspects from either Mars or Saturn, or both, he/she is more likely to be more destructive or work against self development. This then pollutes the influence from the Lunar Nodes.

Next, we consider the North Node, ruled by Venus and Jupiter. If the North Node is favorably aspected by Venus and/or Jupiter, success and development fall easily into place. Let us consider no aspects to the North Node by Venus or Jupiter. This is not so easy for development unless aspected well by the Sun. Naturally the houses in the chart where Venus and Jupiter are located are important to this development. Also aspects to Venus and Jupiter are important as a secondary pattern of experience. The same is true of Mars and Saturn for the South Node with secondary aspects.

The final and overall thing to remember is there is really no pure description of the South and North Node placement by signs. Of course, we have to start with a general description to give a base understanding, like starting with the basic ingredients for a cake. Each South, North Node description would have as many variations as there are stars in the sky or at least as many as people here on this planet Earth.

This is true when describing Sun signs. No two people follow all the descriptions of a given Sun sign. there will be variations. It is a question of priorities, as follows:

#1—South Node, North Node by sign and house—aspects of Nodes to Rulers.

#2—Aspects to Mars and Saturn and placement of Mars and Saturn.

#3—Aspects to Venus and Jupiter and placement of Venus and Jupiter.

#4—Transits and progressions to these points.

It is not a simple matter; it is a series of experiences through a lifetime, a series of events represented by each and every aspect and its influence, an influence that can change by transit and progression.

The person's growth depends upon awareness of each stage of development. Where the South Node is concerned, it is what is given out and how much is given. It seems the more you give, the more you can take in at the North Node (strange to say). If you do not give an adequate measure at the South Node, you do nor take in as much at the North node. Looking at all this is more than just scientific consideration, or theory, much of it is spiritual and in the end it depends upon awareness, dedication, and effort. You either use, it, or it uses you. It is a measure if give and take. The more we are able to give, the more room we seem to have to receive. This seems to be the cosmic law. When we solve the problems of give and take and achieve a balance between the two we finally get at the South Node, turning things around so to speak.

Remember, it is natural for the flow to scatter at the South Node and for the flow to focalize, or singularize and come in a the North Node position, but effort can turn this around. The astronomical description of the Lunar Nodes energy is the natural inclination, but does not mean that mentally and spiritually we cannot turn it around through effort and achieve balance.

The Lunar Nodes are definitely like a whirlpool—especially the South Node because instincts at this point are more unconscious. (The outer planets. Uranus, Neptune and Pluto also share this more unconscious influence.) It takes a conscious will power to be aware of what is happening at the South Node.

If we are to isolate and examine the greatest whirlpool of the chart it is the South Node for it holds us even despite our own will at times. It is a force that never completely leaves us. It always remains our dearest desire. There may be balance at the North Node for life does force experiences of that nature on us for development at that point. However, we may not always desire that development and could give it up all in a second if the whirlpool affect at the South Node offers a chance for temporary focus, like a lorelei.

We are aware of body, mind, and spirit but are we always aware of soul value which can be hidden in its influence. The unconscious we need try to make ourselves aware of.

The force is everywhere present for us, but we do not usually see it unless we are looking for it. Too often we take our conscious self for granted, not looking any deeper and further for potentials of self. The blessings are usually hidden or unconscious and are mixed amidst the ordinary. Jesus said, "Seek and you will find, for every one who asks, receives, and he who seeks, finds. " But we do have to seek. We need to open our eyes and look around. The treasures of full development may already be with you, hidden in the midst of what seems to be ordinary experiences lying dormant. Look deeper into each experience for in it may be the hidden jewel.

Only after our lessons are learned and our teachers are all gone, can we feel secure and confident at both poles of the Nodes. We may give at the South Node position (for life forces us to do this), but do not underestimate a more selfish attitude at this pole for there is much of self in it.

We have to force ourselves either way….a FORCE OF WILL!

www.ingramcontent.com/pod-product-compliance
Ingram Content Group UK Ltd.
Pitfield, Milton Keynes, MK11 3LW, UK
UKHW041422180426
11947UKWH00007B/246